APPLIED LEATHERCRAFT

Applied

Leathercraft

By CHRIS H. GRONEMAN

The MANUAL ARTS PRESS · Peoria, Illinois

Copyright, 1942

CHRIS H. GRONEMAN

No part of this book may be reproduced in any
form without permission of the copyright owner.

34C68

Preface

In this book on one of the most attractive crafts that man has developed, special attention is paid to the many details of leathercraft needed by the beginner if he wishes to produce attractive pieces of work. The most widely accepted processes —including simple but important step-by-step operations such as cutting and skiving, gluing, stitching, decoration, sewing, plaiting, tool selection, and many other factors—are treated thoroughly. Each project is illustrated with a working drawing and photographs that show all the materials used and stages in the making of the article. In addition, the book includes a brief history of leathermaking and man's use of leather.

The projects were chosen for their usefulness, attractiveness, and simplicity, since this book is intended for schools, Scout organizations, summer camps, the home workshop, and similar centers where many of the boys—or girls!—are doing leatherwork for the first time. Therefore full information is repeated with each project, so that the worker may do a complete job without hunting through other books or other parts of this book to find some detail that he has forgotten or never heard of before. To aid activity leaders as well as the worker in find-

5

ing ideas for leather decoration, one section of the book is devoted to design suggestions that have proved very popular among acquaintances of the author and in his leathercraft classes.

In selecting the projects, fundamental examples of leatherwork—key cases, wrist bands, belts, pocketbooks, a notebook, and others—were chosen so that the beginner would gain all-around experience with basic leatherworking problems as a foundation for his future work. In addition, to meet the demand for instructions on the making of Boy Scout accessories, there are such projects as a Scout neckerchief slide, hat bands, an ax sheath, and a knife sheath, together with details on the preparation of leather for such work.

Acknowledgment is gratefully extended to my wife, Virginia, for her criticism and assistance in design, to the Ohio Leather Company, Girard, Ohio, and to the Tanners' Council of America, New York, N. Y., for their permission and splendid cooperation in the use of numerous photographs and informational materials.

—CHRIS H. GRONEMAN

Contents

Foreword

THERE ARE two reasons in particular why this book may be
expected to receive a hearty welcome at this time. First, there
is a marked trend in the direction of emphasis upon develop-
ment of interest in and knowledge about industry in school
shopwork. Material contributing to this end is a distinguishing
feature of the book. Second, there has been in recent years a
notable increase in the use of a considerable variety of printed
and illustrated instruction materials in industrial-arts teaching. The book is a contribution to this desirable trend. Other
cogent reasons could be given if space permitted.

In these directions the author of this book aids the handicraft teacher in the attainment of significant objectives. The
essential facts about the industrial background of leathercraft
are presented in an attractive and authoritative manner. Complete instructions are given for making a progressive series of
projects of excellent design, and everything is beautifully and
fully illustrated.

Here then is a commendable example of the successful
teacher making the results of his experience available to others
and thus contributing to the advancement of the profession.

9

A great deal more of this sort of effort is needed. Too many teachers are teaching this year as they taught ten years ago. Having made no special effort to learn anything new, it seems likely that some of them may have taught themselves out. This would be a stimulating book to fall into the hands of such a one. It would be even more useful in the hands of a wideawake, progressive teacher.

There is another class of readers who will welcome this book; namely, leisure-time, amateur craftsmen. Materials and methods are presented so effectively that the home craftsman who possesses a modest degree of mechanical skill and ingenuity can accomplish worth-while results. This book will provide him with many evenings of fascinating employment.

Kansas State Teachers College, of which Mr. Groneman is an alumnus, is justifiably proud of what he has accomplished, and of the recognition that has come to him for his professional achievements.

—WILLIAM T. BAWDEN

Department of Industrial Education
Kansas State Teachers College
Pittsburg, Kansas

History and Early Uses
of Leather

WHEN PRIMITIVE MAN learned to tie a hard piece of skin around his feet to protect them from stones and thorns, he increased his hunting speed; when he learned to put water in skin bags, he increased his traveling range and freed himself from the necessity of returning to rivers and springs for longer periods of time; and when he learned to hide behind a tough piece of skin, he became a better warrior, more often victorious. Thus one sees the early advantages in the utilization of skins and hides for protection and clothing.

As the knowledge of leather usage increased, tribes made tents, beds, carpets, armor, harness, and shoes out of it. It was also employed for bow strings, shields, fastening for arrow heads on shafts, and ornaments. Later, canoelike boats were built, and drums of leather were used as means of communication.

Articles of leather thirty-three centuries old have been found in Egypt, where it was classed with gold and ivory in value. The Egyptians during Biblical times used leather for sandals, but, since these were very rare and expensive, only the Pharaohs wore them.

The beginnings of recorded history were found on skin rolls which existed in 1500 b. c., and through the years manuscripts written on such parchment have been preserved.

Romans, in the time of Caesar, made wide use of leather, since their methods of tanning were developed to a relatively high degree. They made common use of leather sandals, and, as indication of high rank, a shoe called the "calceus" was worn. The Roman senator of this period wore the high, black calceus laced down the front, while the noble-blooded patricians wore red shoes.

The Roman soldiers wore leather caps as part of their regular equipment.

Marco Polo, the famous world traveler from Venice, returned from China during the thirteenth century and reported that the great war lord, Kublai Khan, lived in leather tents lined with ermine fur. The Chinese of this period also used flexible tanned leather, highly colored and decorated, for bed coverings and dress.

Clothing worn during the fourteenth and fifteenth centuries consisted chiefly of leather doublets and hose, and shoes in fanciful shapes. It was in this period also that bookmaking became a highly developed art, and books were bound with handsomely tooled leather. Likewise, during this period the guilds, which were the forerunners of modern trade unions, were formed. These professional groups exerted a powerful influence on the leather industry. They controlled apprentice training because the masters, who were the craftsmen, selected the boys to be trained in this skill.

Leather played an increasingly important part in the life of the early colonial settlers of America. It was used for leather stockings, knee breeches, jackets, and coats. It was also used for square-toed shoes, saddles, upholstery for chairs, and to take the place of springs in the early coaches.

In this modern time, manufacturers often use exotic designs in their products which are made possible by the use of such leathers as those obtained from snakes, lizards, sharks, and alligators in the making of shoes, luggage, belts, and handbags.

Making Leather

T HERE ARE two types of treatment that skins and hides undergo before they become leather: (1) curing or dressing and (2) tanning. Curing or dressing hides and skins is the lengthy preliminary process in which the skins are prepared for tanning by the removal of all flesh, hair, and foreign particles that would cause the skin to decay before tanning could take place. Curing preserves skins until they can be tanned.

Tanning is the process by which the cured hides and skins are converted into durable and lasting leather through the medium of either vegetable or mineral agents, often referred to as vegetable and "chrome" tanning agents. Whichever method is used will involve the same preliminary steps in curing or dressing.

Early Methods of Preparing and Tanning

The early history of leather making in America falls into two classifications: (1) that method of tanning practiced by the early Indian and (2) that method followed by the early settlers. The leather made by the Indians was known as buckskin tanned, the superior method being that used by the Crow

14

Fig. 1. Indian Women Washing Skins to Remove Flesh and Other Undesirable Matter

Indians. The women of the tribe, Fig. 1, did the work of dressing the skins. This shows them removing flesh and other particles from the hides by washing them in a stream and then
rubbing off the softened impurities.

The following steps in dressing the skins were usually performed: The skins were first piled, wetted, and left for the
period of time necessary for decomposition to set in and loosen
the hair. (The Crow Indian method was superior to this in
that the hides were immersed in a solution of lye water made
from ashes of campfires.) The flesh and hairsides of the skin
were next scraped to remove all foreign matter. They were
then hung in a tightly closed teepee in which a smudge fire
smoked and cured the skins. The leather made by this method
withstood wetting, and, after it dried, returned to its original
soft, pliable condition.

The early settlers in America followed a method of tanning
which had been practiced in Europe for centuries, that of tanning by means of oak bark. In the preliminary steps of dress-

ing the skins, they were soaked in lime and water and then the hair was scraped off. The hides were then laid in crude boxes or vats and sprinkled with ground oak bark until the vat was filled with alternate layers. The hides then soaked for approximately six months.

When it was found that tannin was the ingredient in the oak bark that acted as the tanning agent, other sources of this vegetable product, such as hemlock leaves, nut galls, certain oriental trees, and sumac bark widened the geographical field of tanning, since localities that did not have oak trees could still furnish the raw material, tannin.

Modern Method of Preparation for Tanning

Whether leather is to be tanned by the use of vegetable agents or chrome salts, the preparatory steps in dressing the hides and skins are alike. Modern methods of dressing and curing involve intricate machinery and a high productive efficiency.

When hides and skins are received in a tannery they are immediately placed in cold storage until ready for treatment. The first step in preparing skins and hides for tanning is to wash and clean them until they are soft and free of most of the foreign matter. It is quite often necessary to use chemicals to expedite this operation. Fig. 2 shows hides in soak pits where the chemicals soften dry hides and skins and make it easier to remove the foreign particles.

The soft, flexible stock is now passed through a fleshing machine, which has revolving knives that cut away undesirable foreign matter such as fat and surplus flesh.

Hides and skins now receive further chemical treatment in which hair must be removed. This is accomplished by submerging them in a solution of lime and sodium sulphite. This treatment requires approximately one week.

When the skins and hides have been removed from the solution they go through an unhairing process by machine which

Fig. 2. Soaking Hides and Skins to Remove Dirt, Flesh, and Other Foreign Matter

is similar to the fleshing operation except that it is more thorough. Fig. 3 shows the method of removing all the final traces of hair and epidermis by hand. This is done by placing the skins over beams and cutting away the surplus hair that the machine fails to remove.

Skins must now be treated to a softened condition before they can be tanned. This is carried out in a pickling process, which is a further treatment by chemicals. However, the skins are now too pliable, being very similar to cloth, and they must be worked further in a solution containing sulphuric acid, salt, and water, after which the stock takes on the feel of leather.

These steps complete the essential cleaning and dressing preparation prior to actual tanning.

Chrome Tanning

Chrome-tanned leather is usually used in shoe uppers, gloves, and garments. It is a speedy process by which the dressed skins can be converted into leather in a day's time.

Chrome is derived from the metal chromium, converted by heat and a chemical reaction into bichromate of soda. The crystals thus formed, when treated with suphuric acid and glucose, make a green solution or liquor which is used in chrome tanning.

The dressed skins and hides are put into tanning drums, Fig. 4, which contain the chrome solution. They emerge from these drums with a light bluish color which must be removed by the application of baking soda.

The process of shaving is the next step. This smooths the flesh side of the skin so that it comes out rather uniform in thickness. Fig. 5 shows how the skins are cut to uniform thickness by inserting them between spiral cutting knives on a shaving machine. For skins which are too thick, the stock is split so that an upper side, called the grain, and the reverse side, called the flesh-split, result.

In the event that the leather is to be colored, it is now sent

OHIO LEATHER COMPANY

Fig. 3. Working Skins over Beams by Hand to Remove All Final Traces of Hair Which the Unhairing Machines Failed to Get

Fig. 4. Chrome-tanning Drums Which Revolve to Keep an Even Penetration of the Liquid Through the Skins

20

OHIO LEATHER COMPANY

Fig. 5. Skins Being Shaved between Spiral Cutting Knives to Produce a Uniform Thickness

Fig. 6. Tacking Skins on Frames for Drying

22

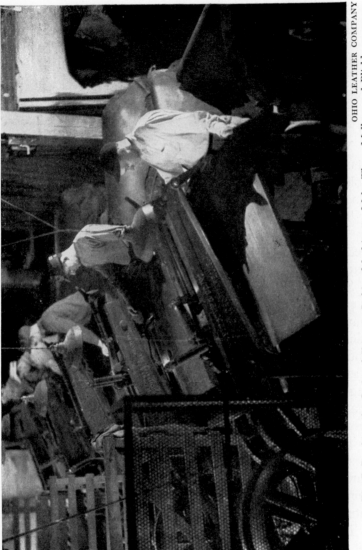

Fig. 7. Breaking the Crust of Skins on Staking Machine to Make Them Mellow and Pliable

23

to the dyeing department. The coloring process and the sub-
sequent oiling cause the stock to emerge very wrinkled; therefore the skins are tacked on frames, Fig. 6, so that they will dry
smoothly.

The skins are next treated in staking machines, Fig. 7, to
break the dried crust and to mellow, preparatory to finishing.

Vegetable Tanning

Vegetable-tanned leathers are used mostly for tooling,
stamping-belt material, luggage, upholstery, harness, and shoe
soles. This process requires a much longer period of time than
does chrome tanning. It usually takes from two to six months.

Tannin, the agent used in this process, is extracted by a
method known as leaching (similar to brewing coffee), from
certain barks, nuts, and leaves. It is then diluted to the desired
strength, in hot water.

Skins and hides, which have been prepared for tanning in
a similar process to that for chrome tanning, are hung on
frames which move back and forth through a solution of tannin liquor. This circulates the solution so that the treatment
and coloring of the skins will be uniform. They are put through
a series of such vats, in each of which the solution is increased
in strength, until the skins are thoroughly saturated. It usually
requires from two to three weeks for the hides to swell properly and become ready for the next treatment.

They are now removed from the frames and placed in lay-
away vats. A layer of skins and hides is covered with ground
bark, to which the tannic acid solution is added. This operation is repeated from four to seven times, requiring two to six
months to secure the desired quality of leather.

The leather is then taken from the vats and put into another
vat filled with hot water, where the excess tanning liquid, sedi-
ment, and bark are washed away. The leather is further cleaned
in a scrubber, to remove all final traces of undesired matter.

Leather becomes very dry after this treatment and must be

OHIO LEATHER COMPANY

Fig. 8. Producing a Glazed Finish by Means of Friction from a Glass Cylinder with Machine Pressure

25

Fig. 9. Producing a Suede Finish on Leather by Working the Skin Against a Buffing Wheel

26

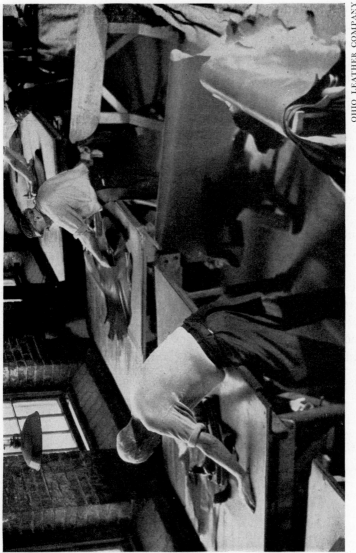

Fig. 10. Hand-rubbing Leather Against Leather to Produce Fancy Grain Effects

given flexibility and life by rubbing it with a natural oil, such as cod oil, a very good lubricant for this purpose. It is then hung in a dark, well-ventilated, humid, drying loft where it dries to the right texture. Skins and hides are now ready for the finishing process.

Finishing of Leathers

Various textures in leather are obtained by glazing, Fig. 8; buffing, Fig. 9; and graining, Fig. 10.

A glazed finish is produced from the friction which results when a glass cylinder rubs over the leather to produce a highly polished, glazed surface, as may be seen in Fig. 8.

A buffed finish is the type found on suede leathers and is produced by buffing wheels, which raise a fine nap on the leather.

A grain finish is usually produced by hand, by working the leather grain to grain, forward and backward, crossing and re-crossing, until the desired effect is produced. Fancy grains are often made by spraying the leathers with various colored solutions. Each of these operations requires expert hand manipulation of each skin to produce the desired product.

Geographical Sources of
Leather

THE UNITED STATES produces approximately 121,000,000 green, salted hides per year from home sources and imports a like number. Hides are imported chiefly from South America, while skins come from the rest of the world, as may be seen by referring to Fig. 11.

The most important source of leather in the United States is cattle hides; 15,000,000 are obtained annually from the home source, while but 5,000,000 are imported, from Canada, Mexico, or Argentina. These hides are produced wherever beef or dairy cattle are raised, and calfskins are obtained from dairy or veal-producing regions. About 14,000,000 calfskins are used per year.

Sheep- and lambskins are obtained from every important country except Japan. About 17,000,000 per year are produced in the United States, while the remaining 18,000,000 are imported. Cabretta skins are interesting because they are termed "haired sheep," due to the fact that the animals resemble sheep

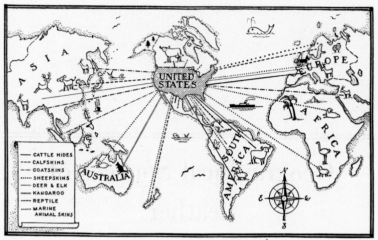

TANNERS' COUNCIL OF AMERICA
Fig. 11. American Tanners Use Hides and Skins from All over the World

but produce hair like goats, instead of wool. About 3,000,000 of these skins are imported each year from Brazil and Africa.

Goat- and kidskins are the most expensive per unit of weight, and also are the most numerous, since each year 50,-000,000 are imported from Europe, Central Africa, South America, India, and China. These countries supply the demand because they use goats for their milk and meat supply.

There are several additional sources of leather which rank next to the foregoing most important ones. They are: pigskins, which are mostly imported from Europe because pigs slaughtered in the United States are not generally skinned; deerskins, which are imported from Latin America and Canada; ostrich skins, the only skin obtained from birds, imported from South Africa; snake- and lizardskins, obtained generally from the python and anaconda snakes, both of which are found in tropical countries; and alligator and crocodile skins, imported from Mexico, Central South America, the Philippine Islands, and Africa. However, some of these skins are found in the bayous of Florida and Louisiana.

Sealskins and walrus skins are brought in from New Foundland, while sharkskins are found in tropical waters, chiefly off the coast of Australia and Lower California.

Horsehides and coltskins come from France, although a limited number are obtained in the United States.

Water-buffalo hides are imported from Southern Asia, and nearly 100,000,000 kangaroo skins are shipped in every year from Australia.

Thus one sees that the sources of general-utility leather lie in the United States, Canada, and Argentina, with the exception of goatskins, which come from the rest of the world. The sources of the rare and more expensive leather are found in far-off and exciting regions of the globe.

Kinds of Art Leather

How to Buy

Pelts of animals fall into two classifications, by name and by condition. The names of pelts are (1) hides, (2) skins, and (3) kips. Hides are obtained from larger animals, such as steers, cows, horses, and walrus; skins are obtained from the smaller animals, such as calves, sheep, goats, and kangaroos; while kips are the pelts of undersized animals. The condition of the pelt is termed (1) green, when it comes directly from the animal; (2) green-salted, when salt has been rubbed on the flesh; (3) dry-salted, after salt has been rubbed in and dried; and (4) dried, after the fresh pelt has been stretched on a board and dried.

The kinds of skins and hides which are suitable for craft- and art-work are:

(1) *Russian, tooling calfskin.* This may be obtained in two grades, A and B. The latter is suitable for beginners, while grade A is recommended for fine-finished projects. Calf has the finest grain of all tooling leathers and is the very best for this purpose. It is offered in a variety of colors.

(2) *Steerhide* may be purchased in two weights, heavy and light. Heavy is $\frac{5}{64}$ inches thick, and the light is $\frac{3}{64}$ inches thick. The lightweight is ideal for billfolds and other small projects; the heavy is more suited for brief cases, notebook covers, and similar large projects. This hide is excellent for tooling yet makes up well in a plain design because of the crinkle-grained finish. Commercial manufacturers now have steerhide dyed in mottled effect with such three-toned combinations as red, green, and brown. This finish is beautiful and durable.

(3) *Cowhides* are classified as (a) tooling, which can be tooled; (b) stamping or carving; and (c) nontooling. They are also listed according to weight, heavy and light. Heavyweight, tooling cowhide is excellent for belts and ax sheaths. When purchasing it for belts, shoulder pieces should be bought because these pieces are the most suitable with the least amount of defective leather. Cowhide has a soft finish and is sold in only a few colors, natural being most popular.

(4) *Pigskin* in the best grade is usually imported. These skins are graded according to uniformity of thickness and texture. Pigskin is toolable, but the interesting texture makes it a most desirable material in its natural state. It is ideal for any of the smaller projects, since it is rather expensive.

(5) *Sheepskin* is sold in one grade and is a good substitute for a tooling material because it is inexpensive. Sheepskin is durable and tools without difficulty. Its colors are usually limited to natural and black; but the natural dyes beautifully.

(6) *Suede* (lamb- or sheepskin) is a nontooling leather which is ideal for purses and other small projects, and because of its soft, velvet finish it is also an excellent lining leather. Suede sheepskin may be obtained in a variety of colors.

(7) *Alligator* or *lizard*, grain leather is a nontooling leather but is one which is very attractive because of the surface decoration embossed by the manufacturer. It is a very strong and handsome leather, suitable for most projects. It is available in a variety of colors and is relatively inexpensive.

(8) *Chrome-tanned calfskin* is a nontooling leather which is excellent for lining purses and handbags. It is inexpensive and available in a few colors, including black and brown.

(9) *Skivers* are thin, split-off parts of thick hides and skins which are used only for lining. They are least expensive, available in either a smooth or rough finish and various colors.

(10) *Lacing* may be purchased either by the yard or made with the use of a thong cutter. The latter is recommended only for use on knife and ax sheaths. Lacing comes in two forms, round and flat. The round style makes very attractive, braided articles, while the flat, usually $3/32$ inches wide, has beveled edges suitable for lacing. For the amateur or beginner, it is suggested that an imitation lacing be used. This is often known under such trade-names as "craft strip," "artisan-lace," "pyro-lace," and other similar names. Goatskin or calfskin lacing is preferable, but it is more expensive than imitations. When using wide lacing for the Venetian stitch, on large projects such as notebooks and brief cases, the lace can be made from skiver leather by using the thong cutter.

Leather may be purchased in several ways:

(1) *Full hides* or *skins*—this is the most economical method when purchasing large quantities of leather.

(2) *Half skins, half hides,* or *quarter skins*—this description is self-explanatory, in that whole skins and hides are cut according to sections given, at slightly higher cost.

(3) *Square foot* or *square inch*—this is the ideal method to buy small pieces for one or two small projects. The cost is almost prohibitive when ordering in large quantities.

(4) *Scrap leather* or *remnants*—this method is preferred by many for beginning students or for making many small projects. Scraps are usually sold by the one- or five-pound lots.

(5) *Leathercraft kits*—ready-cut pieces; lace, instructional material, and all necessary accessories for the particular project complete such a kit. Many teachers desire this method of buying leather when working with a small group of students.

Suggested Projects

Leather projects are many and varied; some are very simple, and others involve difficult operations. The following lists present a small selection of worthwhile projects from which the novice or expert may select those which interest him most and which are suitable for his activities.

The operations discussed are ample to carry the worker through the steps needed in making most of the listed projects.

BOY SCOUT PROJECTS

archery equipment
ax sheaths
belts
billfolds
comb cases
canteen cases
dog collars and leads
first-aid cases
hatbands
holsters
hunting-license cases
identification-card cases
key cases

knife sheaths
lanyards
match cases
moccasins
neckerchief slides
photograph albums
quirts
sandals
stamp books
watch fobs
wrist supports
wrist-watch straps

MISCELLANEOUS PROJECTS

automobile drivers' license cases
billfolds
book covers
book ends
bookmarks
brief cases
bridge-set cases
camera cases
cigarette cases
coin purses
comb cases
desk sets
gloves
handbags
hand purses
handkerchief cases
key containers
letter holders
match-box covers

memorandum cases
moccasins
music cases
napkin rings
notebook covers
pencil-and-pen cases
photograph albums
photograph folders
playing-card cases
sandals
stamp books
suspenders
table runners
telephone-book covers
tobacco pouches
toilet-set cases
wall hangings
whisk-broom holders
wrist-watch straps

Essential Tools

Tools for leather work are relatively inexpensive when compared with the cost of tools for other divisions of industrial arts, or equipment for the home craftsman, or when compared with the value of the product made. It will be noted from the panel photograph, Fig. 12, and the discussion in the listing of the tools, that many of the essential tools are common to other activities; hence they will already be available in the shop inventory, or among the tools of the home workman.

Such tools as the junior steel square (5), shoe polisher (14), dye brush (18), awl (20), or mallet (13) may be procured at a minimum cost from a local variety or ten-cent store. A few of the tools may easily be made in the school or home workshop. These are so indicated in the following listing of tools (the numbers indicated for each tool in the list correspond to those in Fig. 12):

No. 1. Lacing gauge punch—to punch holes for lacing, buckles, snap attachments, and adjustment holes on belts. Revolving punches are available in either four or six tube sizes. The four-tube, revolving punch, Fig. 13, has a thumbscrew adjustment for spacing. This adjustment is not standard with all

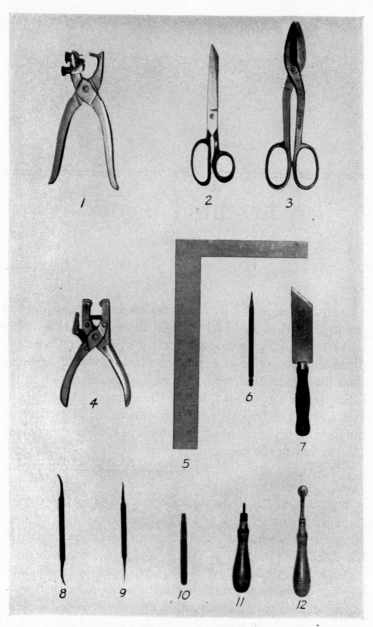

Fig. 12. Leatherworking Tools

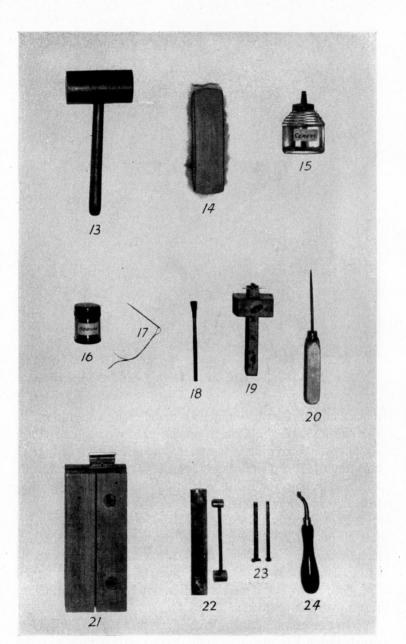

(Fig. 12 continued)

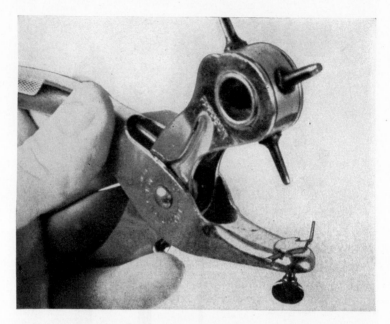

Fig. 13. Four-Tube Revolving, Lacing Gauge Punch with Space Gauge

makes, and this tool should be ordered from a source which specifies it. A one-hole gauge punch, however, is satisfactory, if the correct-size tube is supplied. The one shown in Fig. 14 has a depth gauge as well as a hole-spacing gauge. A punch with both adjustments is highly desirable for beginners. The additional cost for gauges is slight.

2. *Scissors*—to cut leather and paper templates. Scissors for this purpose should be heavy duty, ten inches or longer. They should be made of high-grade steel so that a sharp edge is easily maintained.

3. *Snips*—to cut cowhide and metal templates. Ordinary tin snips are satisfactory.

4. *Eyelet-setting punch*—to punch holes and set eyelets which fasten key plates securely. Eyelet-setting units may be had which fit the lacing gauge punch.

5. *Junior steel square*—to measure straight-line marking and general layout work.

6. *Pencil*—to trace designs from original drawings and for other pencilwork.

7. *Skiving knife*—for skiving edges and for splicing lace. This knife can be made from a discarded cobbler's knife.

8. *Tracer and spoon modeler*—for general, outline tooling and background modeling. This tool can be made from an ordinary ice pick when only a tracer is needed.

9. *Tracer and deerfoot modeler*—for general, outline tooling and intricate background modeling.

10. *Edge creaser*—to crease a line parallel to any edge. This tool can be made from hardwood. Often this tool is listed as a metal tool.

11. *Multipointed stippler*—to stipple designs or backgrounds.

12. *Embossing wheel and carriage*—to emboss designs on

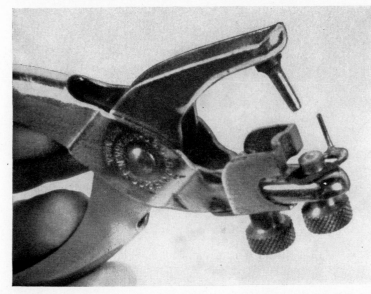

Fig. 14. Single-Tube Lacing Gauge Punch with Space and Depth Gauges

borders. Interchangeable embossing wheels of various designs are available.

13. *Mallet*—for stamping designs, setting snaps, and general utility. It can be made from any of the hardwoods.

14. *Polisher*—for final polishing of the project. An ordinary shoe polisher is excellent.

15. *Cement bottle and applier*—to keep rubber cement ready for application. A discarded paste jar with a rubber spatula is satisfactory.

16. *Dye container*—for keeping dye. Ordinary ink bottles are adequate.

17. *Stitching needle*—for stitching or hand sewing.

18. *Dye brush*—for applying dye to edges. Water-color brushes are ideal.

19. *Draw gauge*—to cut belts and various straps. This tool may be purchased or can easily be made from a discarded woodwork-marking gauge as illustrated in Fig. 15. The cutting

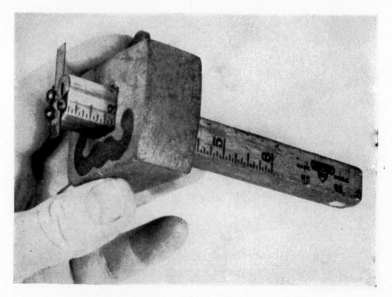

Fig. 15. Draw Gauge Made from Marking Gauge

Fig. 16. Thong Cutter Using Razor Blade

knife is a razor blade which is attached to the end of the gauge with screws.

20. *Awl or fid*—for piercing and marking. An ice pick may be used.

21. *Thong cutter*—to cut thong of various widths. Fig. 16 shows a unique cutter which may be made. All that is needed is a wood block, size 1¼ x 4 x 6 inches, with a saw cut or kerf lengthwise on the face side to a depth of ⅝ inch. A razor blade pressed in the end grain will cut and at the same time determine the width of the thong. See p. 166.

22. *Snap-setting outfit*—for setting and fastening snap buttons.

23. *Stamping tools*—for stamping backgrounds in various designs. These tools can be made from 16- and 20-penny nails. The designs illustrated in Fig. 17 can be duplicated on the heads of nails by using machine and jewelers' files, a fine-cutting grinding wheel, and drill bits.

24. *Metal, single-edge creaser*—ideal for edge-creasing belts and other heavy material.

Dividers or compass (not illustrated)—for stepping off equal distances and marking disks for thong cutting.

Tooling and stamping block (not illustrated)—to tool or stamp leather on. A piece of close-grained hardwood measur-

STAMPING DESIGNS

Fig. 17. Stamping Designs, Reproduced Half Size

ing ¾ x 6 x 10 inches is a convenient-size block. A slab of marble is preferable to wood because it will not dent. Marble can often be purchased at used-furniture stores at a nominal cost.

Templates, Fig. 18—for permanent patterns. Paper or cardboard templates are adequate but those cut from sheet metal are more satisfactory and permanent.

Portable tool-and-supply cabinet—for storage of leathercraft tools and various small supplies. Fig. 19 shows the tool cabinet closed and ready to be carried to any desired work center. Fig. 20 pictures the cabinet open with a possible tool arrangement. The center compartment is for the storage of leather designs and has drawer space for various special items such as snap buttons, belt buckles, key rings, and key plates.

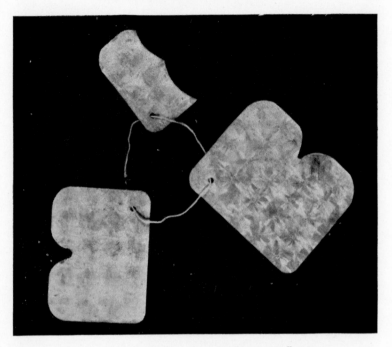

Fig. 18. Sheet-Metal Templates for Permanent Patterns

Fig. 19. Portable Tool Cabinet Closed

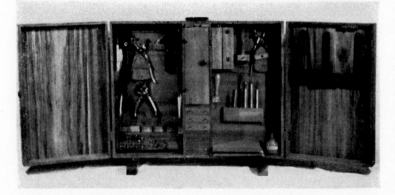

Fig. 20. Portable Tool Cabinet Open

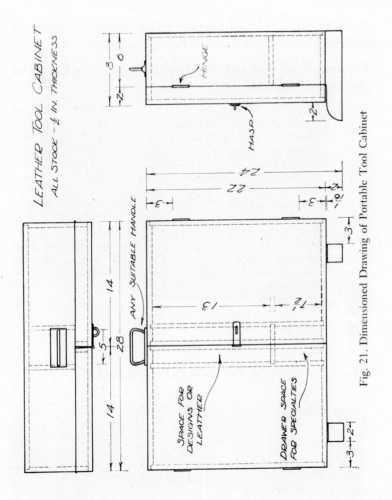

LEATHER TOOL CABINET
ALL STOCK - ½ IN. THICKNESS

ANY SUITABLE HANDLE

SPACE FOR DESIGNS OR LEATHER

DRAWER SPACE FOR SPECIALTIES

HINGE

HASP

Fig. 21. Dimensioned Drawing of Portable Tool Cabinet

Fig. 21 is a dimensioned drawing giving suggested sizes for a portable cabinet which is ample for the average-size class.

Minimum Tool List and Approximate Cost for a Group of Six to Ten Students

Quantity	Item		Unit Cost	Total Cost
1	Lacing gauge punch with guides	(1)*	$1.20	$1.20
1	Heavy-duty scissors, 10 in.	(2)	1.25	1.25
1	Junior steel square	(5)	.15	.15
1	Skiving knife	(7)	.35	.35
4	Tracer and spoon modelers	(8)	.40	1.60
1	Edge creaser	(10)	.15	.15
1	Sheepskin polisher	(14)	.10	.10
1	Dye brush	(18)	.05	.05
1	Snap-setting outfit	(22)	1.00	1.00
1	Awl	(20)	This and remaining items	
2	Wooden mallets	(13)	can be made or easily ac-	
1	Cement bottle and applier	(15)	quired without cost.	
1	Dye container	(16)		
1	Large needle	(17)		
1	Thong cutter	(21)		
6	Stamping tools of various designs	(23)		
6	Pencils	(6)		

Asterisk (*) indicates number on the photograph of tools, Fig. 12.

1.

Comb Case

THE STUDENT or novice would do well to begin leatherwork with this case because of its usefulness and simplicity and the some twenty fundamental operations embodied in the problem. If the steps presented are followed intelligently, the workman may proceed more confidently with other projects.

Fig. 22. Completed Comb Case

Materials required (Fig. 24):

Quantity	Material	Size
2	Tooling calfskin or mottled steerhide	$1\frac{5}{8}$ x $5\frac{1}{2}$
1	Edge lace—bevel edge	$\frac{3}{32}$ x 30
	Dye (India ink)	
	Rubber cement	
	Saddle soap	

49

COMB CASE

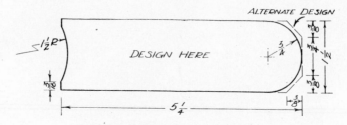

ALTERNATE DESIGN

$1\frac{1}{2}R$

DESIGN HERE

$\frac{3}{4}$

$5\frac{1}{4}$

$\frac{3}{8}$

Fig. 23. Working Drawing for Comb Case

Essential tools (the numbers below indicate tools shown in Fig. 12):

cement applier (15), dye brush (18), edge creaser (10), lacing gauge punch (1), paper clips, pencil (6), scissors (2), skiving knife (7), sheepskin polisher (14), sponge, straightedge, and tracer modeling tool (8).

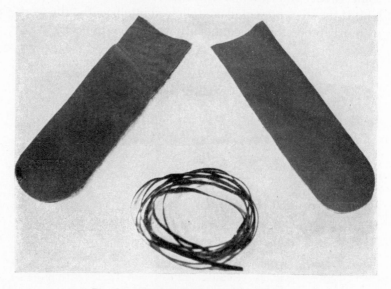

Fig. 24. Materials Required for Comb Case

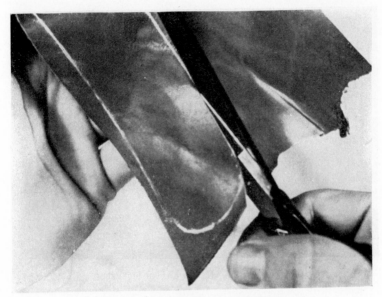

Fig. 25. Cutting Leather with Scissors

Order of procedure:

(1) Draw and cut out the pattern. See Fig. 23 for dimensions.

(2) Place the pattern on the smooth side of the leather and mark around it with sharp pencil or awl.

(3) Remove the pattern and cut out the pieces carefully on the outlines with sharp scissors, Fig. 25.

(4) Mark the exact size of the cut-out piece of leather on durable tracing paper. Paper should be larger than the cut leather.

(5) Select or create an appropriate design. Refer to the section on Designs, at the back of the book.

(6) Trace or draw the selected design on the tracing paper, Fig. 26.

(7) Moisten the reverse or rough side of the leather with a damp sponge, Fig. 27. Leather should not be saturated with water.

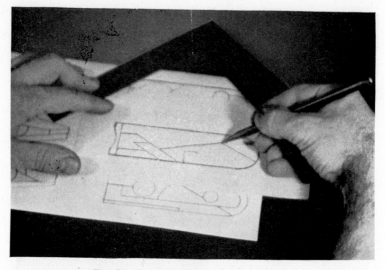

Fig. 26. Tracing Design on Tracing Paper

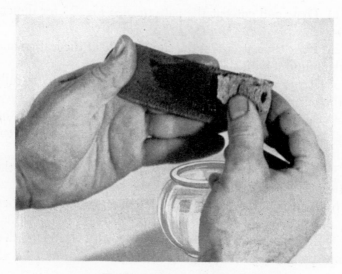

Fig. 27. Moistening Leather for Tooling

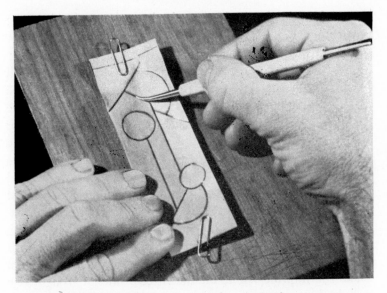

Fig. 28. Tracing the Design on the Leather

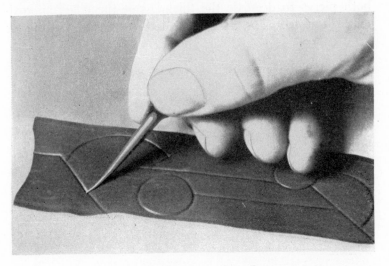

Fig. 29. Pressing Pattern Lines Deeper

(8) Clip the design sheet on the face or smooth side of the cut leather, Fig. 28.

(9) Press the design firmly with the modeling tracer, Fig. 28, which is held at a 45-degree angle so that the imprint will be visible on the leather. It is essential that the leather be

Fig. 30. Imprint Made by Tracer Modeler, Enlarged

placed on some hard surface such as hardwood, marble, or plate glass. This simple type of tooling is known as outline tooling, and is recommended for the beginner as the first step in actual tooling.

(10) Remove the tracing paper and press the pattern lines deeper into the leather with a modeling tracer. The pressure should be great enough to make the imprint visible on the reverse side. A straightedge will facilitate accurate, straight-line work. Refer to Figs. 29 and 30.

(11) Skive the edges of the reverse side of the leather on both pieces to decrease the thickness at the edges approximately one half, Fig. 31. Skiving is the process of paring or

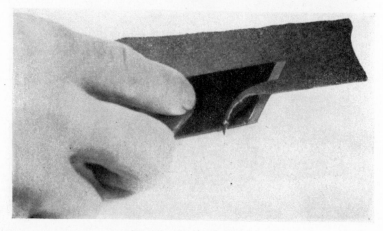

Fig. 31. Skiving the Edges

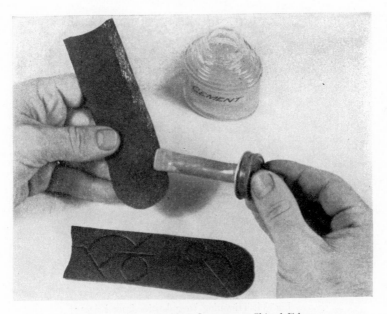

Fig. 32. Applying Rubber Cement on Skived Edges

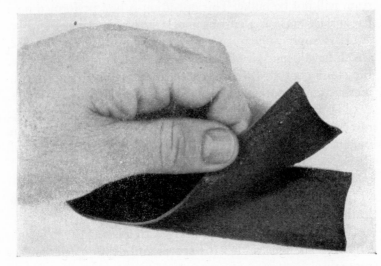

Fig. 33. Pressing Together Cemented Pieces

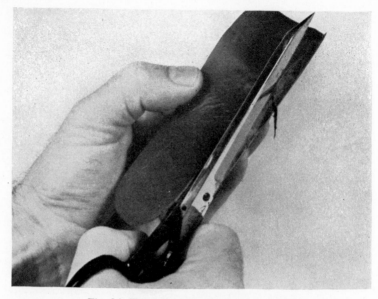

Fig. 34. Trimming Irregularities from Edges

shaving the edges so that when the two pieces are cemented the seam will not be bulky. This operation is best performed on a flat surface such as a cutting block or marble slab.

(12) Apply rubber cement along the inside edges, Fig. 32, which have been skived. *Do not cement the top edges where the comb goes in.* Rubber cement may be procured from numerous craft companies or from any local shoe-repair shops.

(13) Press the pieces together firmly, Fig. 33. The purpose of cementing pieces is to prevent slipping when the holes are punched and laced. Cementing is merely a temporary adhesive.

(14) Trim irregularities from the edges.

(15) Color the edges with India ink the same color as the leather, probably brown, Fig. 35.

(16) Punch the edges for lacing with a lacing gauge punch, Fig. 36, making sure that the spacer and depth gauges are set properly.

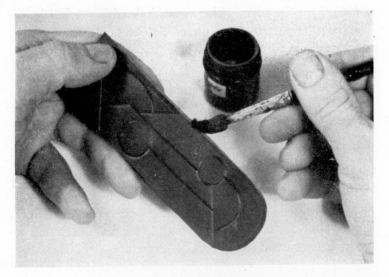

Fig. 35. Coloring the Edges with India Ink

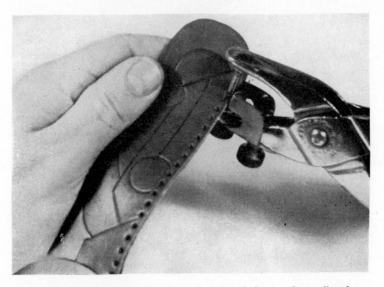

Fig. 36. Punching Holes for Edge Lacing with Lacing Gauge Punch

(17) Lace the edges with a very simple whip stitch, Fig. 37. The length of lace for this stitch is determined by multiplying the distance to be laced by three.

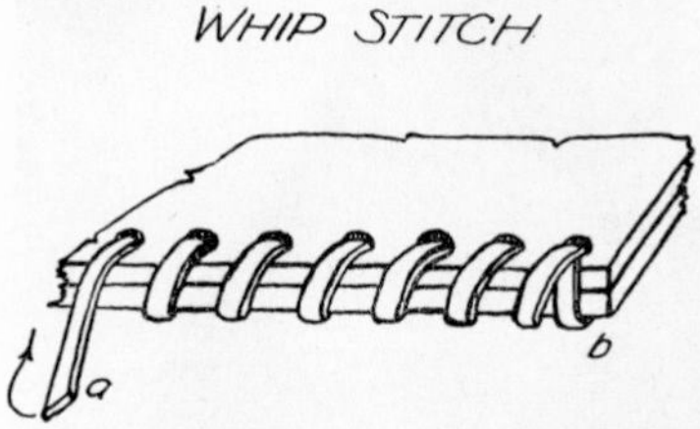

WHIP STITCH

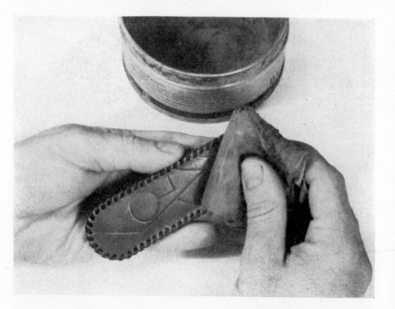

Fig. 37. Design of the Whip Stitch

(a) Start the whip stitch with one end of the lace inserted between the pieces of leather as shown at *b*, Fig. 37.

(b) Thread the lace through the first hole a second time to form a double whip, which acts as a self-fastener.

(c) Proceed with the stitch in the adjacent hole as shown.

(d) To fasten the lacing, double the last stitch and insert between the two pieces of leather.

Fig. 38. Applying Saddle Soap on the Comb Case

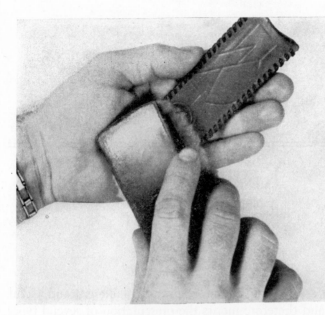

Fig. 39. Polishing the Case

(18) Apply a coat of saddle soap to clean and wax the case, Fig. 38.

(19) Polish the comb case with a sheepskin polisher, Fig. 39.

2.

Key Containers

A KEY CONTAINER is a universally acceptable gift and useful project, and therefore merits the presentation of several types from which to choose. These containers range in difficulty from the simple binding-post containers to the more difficult ones involving the key plate and the zipper fastening.

The first three types are very popular for carrying automobile keys, as they have a capacity of usually only two or three keys. They are inexpensive because the cover can be made of scrap material.

This division presents a variety of key containers which are ideal for either men or women. The key container and coin purse involve many operations from the simplest to the more complex, and the natural advantages are twofold—a desirable project and the mastery of more complicated processes or operations.

To make the zipper-pull, it is necessary to study the operations involving the round thong wherein this particular type of thong work is illustrated and described. This is well worth the additional time entailed. See p. 164.

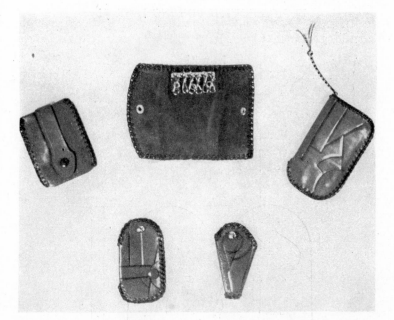

Fig. 40. Group Picture of Key Containers

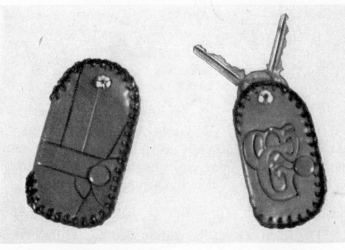

Fig. 41. Key Container with Binding Post #1

KEY CASE WITH BINDING POST #1

Materials required (Fig. 43):

Quantity	Material	Size
1	Tooling calfskin or mottled steerhide	3½ x 3⅞
1	Edge lace—bevel edge	³⁄₃₂ x 80
1	Key-case binding post	Standard
1	Snap-button assembly	⅜
	India ink	
	Rubber cement	
	Saddle soap	

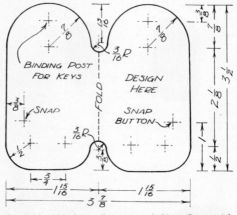

KEY CASE WITH BINDING POST

Fig. 42. Working Drawing of Key Case with
Binding Post

Essential tools (Fig. 12):

cement applier (15), dye brush (18), lacing gauge punch (1), mallet (13), paper clips, pencil (6), scissors (2), sheepskin polisher (14), sponge, snap-setting outfit (22), tracer and deerfoot modeler (9), and waxing cloth.

Order of procedure:

(1) Draw and cut out the pattern. See Fig. 42 for dimensions.

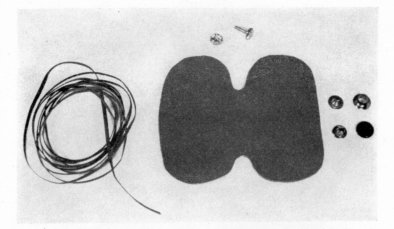

Fig. 43. Materials Required for Key Case

(2) Transfer pattern to smooth side of leather and mark around with sharp pencil or awl.

(3) Remove pattern and cut out piece on the outline with sharp scissors, Fig. 25.

(4) Mark size of cut-out leather on tracing paper.

(5) Select or create appropriate design. Just a letter or monogram usually will suffice for small articles.

(6) Trace or draw design on tracing paper, Fig. 26.

(7) Moisten reverse side of leather, Fig. 27.

(8) Transfer design to leather, Fig. 28.

(9) Remove tracing paper and press pattern lines in.

(10) Decorate design with deerfoot modeler, Figs. 44 and 45. Fig. 45 should be contrasted with Fig. 30 for the difference in modeling. This process is called flat modeling, as the design is brought into relief by pressing down the background around it. This type modeling should have the design so thoroughly embedded into the leather that the reverse side is also clearly marked as in Fig. 51.

(11) Punch the edges for lacing with a lacing gauge punch, Fig. 36. To avoid uneven spacing of the last few holes, disre-

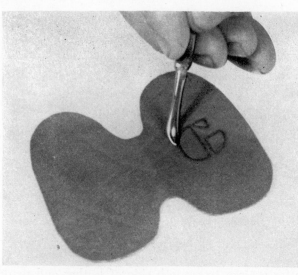

Fig. 44. Flat Modeling with Deerfoot Modeler

gard the spacing gauge on the punch, and space by good judge-
ment.

(12) Color the edges with India ink, Fig. 35.

(13) Lace the edges with the buttonhole stitch, Figs. 46,

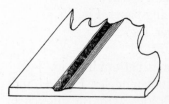

Fig. 45. Imprint Made by Flat
Modeling

47, 48, and 49. This type lacing
is slightly more difficult than the
whip stitch but is more ornamental and is widely used commercially. The length of lace for
this stitch is determined by multiplying the distance to be laced
by five.

(a) Insert the lace through one hole, Figs. 46 and 48–A.

(b) Pass the long part of the lace counterclockwise behind and around the short end of the lace, Figs. 47 and 48–B.

(c) Insert the lace at back side of next hole to the right,
and pull it through, Fig. 48–C.

Fig. 46. Starting the Buttonhole Stitch

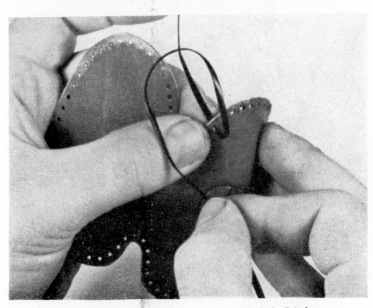

Fig. 47. Forming the Loop in the Buttonhole Stitch

(d) Pass the lace once again counterclockwise back and under the loop left by the last operation, Figs. 48–C and 48–D.

(e) Continue these steps until the project is laced or until a splice is necessary. If the lace must be spliced see operation (14), p. 67.

(f) To fasten the ends, after the lacing has been completed, open or loosen the first two or three stitches on the inside of the case, Fig. 49–A.

BUTTONHOLE STITCH

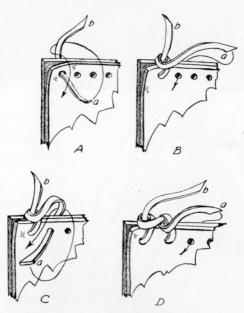

Fig. 48. Details of Buttonhole Stitch Procedure

(g) Apply a small amount of rubber cement on one end of the lace and slip it under the loosened stitches, Fig. 49–B. Treat end b of lace similarly but insert it under the loosened stitches on the other side, in the opposite direction.

(14) If the lace should tear or additional lace be necessary, the following steps of skiving and fastening can be followed, Figs. 50 and 51:

END FASTENING

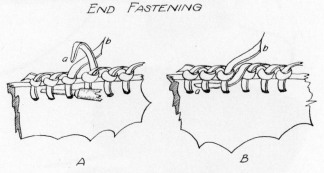

A   B

Fig. 49. Details of End Fastening

SKIVED LACE SPLICE

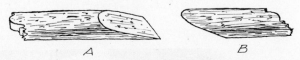

A   B

Fig. 50. Detail of Skiving Edge Lacing

(a) With a skiving knife, skive or thin the ends of the lace to be joined, as in Fig. 31.

(b) Apply rubber cement to the skived faces and allow to stand one minute or longer.

(c) Press the cemented faces together firmly, Fig. 51.

(15) Lay the project on a flat surface and roll the lacing lightly with a mallet, Fig. 52. This is to reduce the bulky appearance and smooth out the lacing.

(16) Mark location for snap-button assembly. Measurement may be found on the working drawing, Fig. 42.

(17) Punch the holes for fastening the eyelet to the cap and for fastening the spring to the post, Fig. 53.

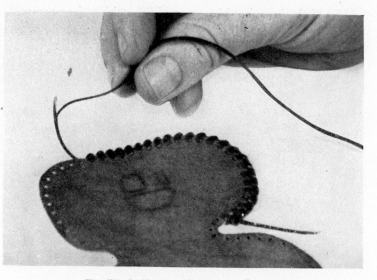

Fig. 51. Cementing Edge Lacing Together

Fig. 52. Rolling the Edge Lacing for Smoothness and Uniformity

Fig. 53. Punching Holes for Snap-Button Assembly

(18) Assemble the snap button, Figs. 54, 55, 56, 57, and 58.

(a) Insert the eyelet and place the cap in position.
(b) Rivet the cap to the eyelet, Figs. 55 and 58.
(c) Insert the post and place the spring in position, Figs. 56 and 58.
(d) Rivet the spring to the post, Figs. 57 and 58.
(e) Fasten the snap button. In the event that too much drive was applied, it may be necessary to pinch the spring with a pliers so that the assembly will work easily.

(19) Snap the key container and mark it for the binding post. Measurements are on the working drawing, Fig. 42.
(20) Punch the hole for the binding post, Fig. 53.
(21) Insert the post and screw the cap on.
(22) Clean with saddle soap and wax, Fig. 38.
(23) Polish the key case, Fig. 39.

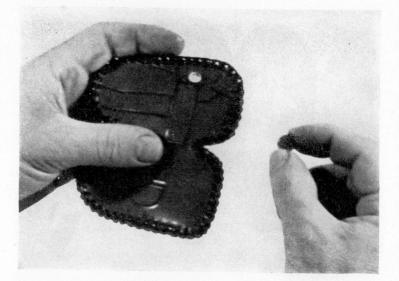

Fig. 54. Placing Cap on Eyelet

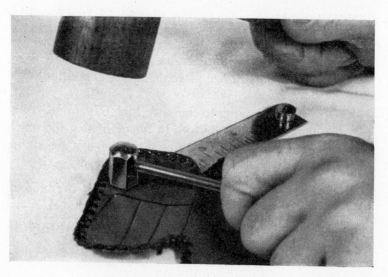

Fig. 55. Riveting Cap to Eyelet

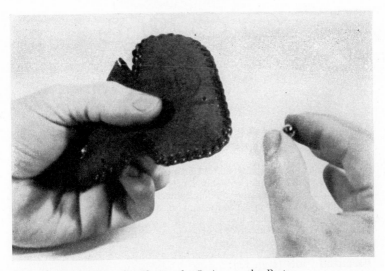

Fig. 56. Placing the Spring on the Post

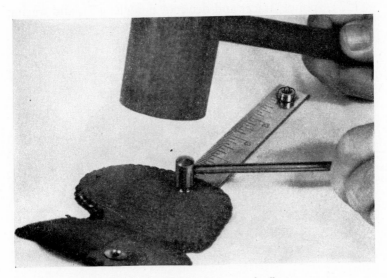

Fig. 57. Riveting the Spring to the Post

CAP EYELET SPRING POST

Fig. 58. Parts of the Snap-Button Assembly

KEY CASE WITH BINDING POST #2

Materials required (Fig. 61):

Quantity	Material	Size
1	Tooling calfskin or mottled steerhide	3½ x 4
1	Edge lace—bevel edge	³⁄₃₂ x 54
1	Key-case binding post	Standard
1	Snap-button assembly	⅜
	India ink	
	Rubber cement	
	Saddle soap	

Essential tools (Fig. 12):

cement applier (15), dye brush (18), lacing gauge punch (1), mallet (13), multipointed stippler (11), paper clips, scissors (2), sheepskin polisher (14), snap-setting outfit (22), sponge, tracer and deerfoot modeler (9), and waxing cloth.

Fig. 59. Key Case with Binding Post #2

KEY CASE WITH BINDING POST

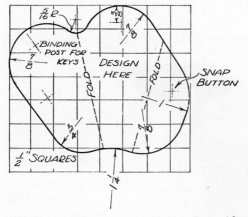

Fig. 60. Working Drawing for Key Case with
Binding Post

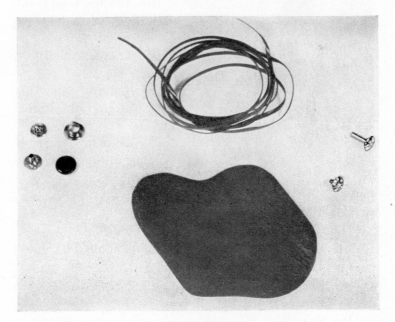

Fig. 61. Materials Required for Key Case

Order of procedure:

(1) Draw and cut out the pattern. See Fig. 60 for dimensions.

(2) Transfer pattern to smooth side of leather and mark around with sharp pencil or awl.

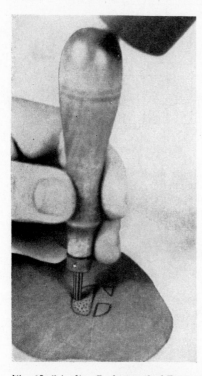

(3) Remove pattern and cut out piece on the outline with sharp scissors, Fig. 25.

(4) Mark size of cut-out leather on durable tracing paper.

(5) Select or create appropriate design and draw on paper, Fig. 26.

(6) Moisten reverse side of leather for tooling, Fig. 27.

(7) Transfer design to leather, Fig. 28.

(8) Remove paper and press pattern into leather, Fig. 29.

(9) Decorate design by stippling in the background, Fig. 62.

Fig. 62. Stippling Background of Design

(10) Punch the edges for lacing with a lacing gauge punch, Fig. 36.

(11) Color the edge with India ink, Fig. 35.

(12) Lace the edge with the buttonhole stitch, Figs. 46–49.

(13) Tap or roll lacing lightly, Fig. 52.

(14) Mark location of snap-button assembly.

(15) Assemble snap button, Figs. 54–58.

(16) Snap the key container and mark for binding post.

Fig. 63. Completed Key-Ring Holder

(17) Punch the hole for binding post, Fig. 53.

(18) Insert post and screw the cap on.

(19) Apply coat of saddle soap and polish, Figs. 38 and 39.

KEY-RING HOLDER

Materials required (Fig. 65):

Quantity	Material	Size
1	Tooling calfskin or mottled steerhide A	2½ x 7
1	Tooling calfskin or mottled steerhide B	1 x 5¾
	Thread—mercerized	No. 40
1	Snap-button assembly	⅜
1	Key ring	1¼
1	Edge lace—bevel edge	³⁄₃₂ x 36
	India ink	
	Rubber cement	
	Saddle soap	

Essential tools (Fig. 12):

awl or fid (20), cement applier (15), dye brush (18), edge creaser (10), lacing gauge punch (1), mallet (13), needle

(17), paper clips, scissors (2), sheepskin polisher (14), snap-setting outfit (22), sponge, tracer and deerfoot modeler (9), and waxing cloth.

Order of Procedure:

(1) Draw and cut out the pattern. See Fig. 64 for dimensions.

(2) Place pattern on smooth side of leather and mark around with sharp pencil or awl.

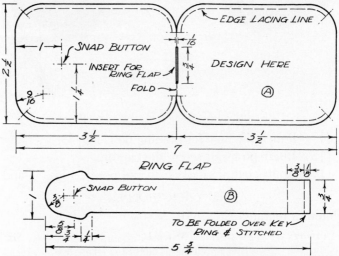

Fig. 64. Working Drawing for Key-Ring Holder

(3) Remove pattern and cut out leather on the outline with sharp scissors, Fig. 25.

(4) Mark size of cut-out leather on durable tracing paper.

(5) Select or create appropriate design. See section on Designs, at the back of the book.

(6) Trace or draw design on paper, Fig. 26.

(7) Moisten reverse or rough side of leather for tooling, Fig. 27.

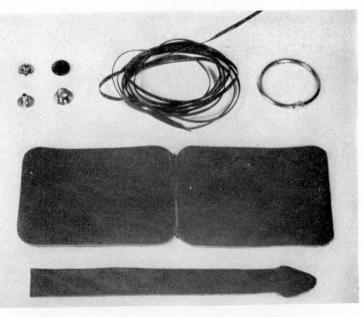

Fig. 65. Materials Required for Key-Ring Holder

(8) Transfer design to leather, Fig. 28.

(9) Remove tracing paper and press pattern lines into leather, Fig. 29.

(10) Decorate the design with the deerfoot modeler, Figs. 44 and 45, or by stippling, Fig. 62.

(11) Mark location on A for ring flap B. See Fig. 64 for measurements.

(12) Cut slit for ring flap as follows (Figs. 66 and 67):

(a) Punch holes for cutting the slit which takes the ring flap, Fig. 66.

(b) Complete the slit by widening it to the diameter of the holes, which will equal the thickness of piece B, Fig. 67.

(13) Crease the edges of piece B, and the edges on A which will not be laced, with an edge creaser, Fig. 68. This operation makes a neater appearance possible.

Fig. 66. Punching Holes for Cutting Slit

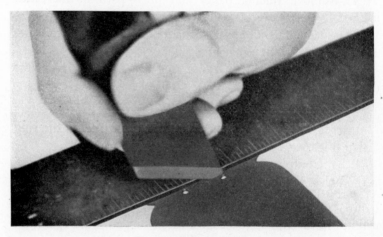

Fig. 67. Cutting the Slit

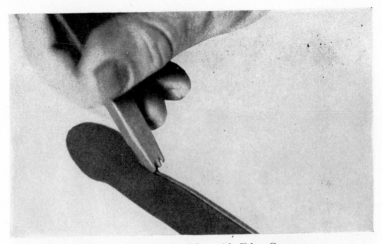

Fig. 68. Creasing the Edge with Edge Creaser

(14) Slip the ring flap B into the slit. Make sure the ring flap will fold correctly on the case when in place.

(15) Place the key ring on the ring flap between the dotted lines, as indicated in Fig. 64.

(16) Sew the ring flap to hold the key ring, Figs. 69, 70, and 71. Proceed as follows:

(a) Apply rubber cement on the inside portion of B, which folds over the ring, Fig. 32.

(b) Perforate the folded leather in a straight line for sewing, Fig. 69. Use an awl or fid.

(c) Sew the leather either by machine or by hand, Figs. 70 and 71, using the cobbler's stitch, Fig. 71. This is merely an in-and-out running stitch sewn in a continuous line.

(17) Skive the edges which are to be laced, Fig. 31.

(18) Apply rubber cement along the skived edges, Fig. 32.

(19) Fold the case and press the cemented edges firmly together, Fig. 33.

(20) Trim irregularities off to assure even edge, Fig. 34.

(21) Color the edges with India ink, Fig. 35.

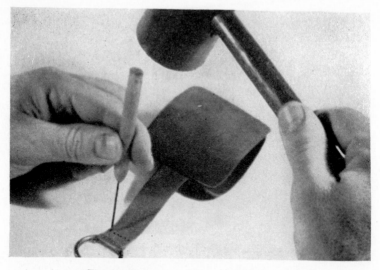

Fig. 69. Perforating with an Awl for Sewing

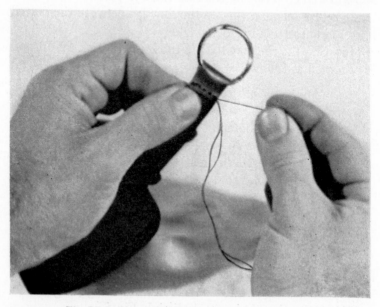

Fig. 70. Sewing by Hand, Using the Cobbler's Stitch

(22) Punch the edges for lacing with lacing gauge punch.

(23) Lace the edges with the buttonhole stitch, Figs. 46–49, or with the whip stitch, Fig. 37.

(24) Tap or roll the edge lacing lightly, Fig. 52.

(25) Mark location for snap-button assembly. See Fig. 64 for measurements.

(26) Punch holes and assemble snap button, Figs. 54–58.

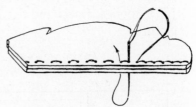

COBBLER'S STITCH

Fig. 71. Detail of the Cobbler's Stitch

(27) Apply coat of saddle soap and polish, Figs. 38 and 39.

KEY CONTAINER WITH KEY PLATE

Materials required (Fig. 74):

Quantity	Material	Size
1	Tooling calfskin or mottled steerhide	4 x 6⅛
1	Skiver lining	4 x 6
1	Scrap leather (plate reinforcement)	1 x 2
1	Edge lace—bevel edge	³⁄₃₂ x 96
1	Key plate	6-hook
1	Snap-button assembly	⅜
3	Eyelets	To fit key plate

India ink; Rubber cement; Saddle soap

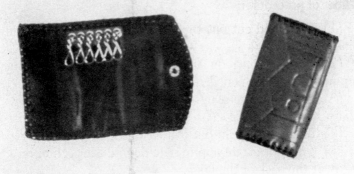

Fig. 72. Open and Closed Key Containers with Key Plates

Essential tools (Fig. 12):

cement applier (15), dye brush (18), eyelet setting punch (4), lacing gauge punch (1), mallet (13), paper clips, scissors (2), sheepskin polisher (14), snap-setting outfit (22), sponge, tracer and deerfoot modeler (9), and waxing cloth.

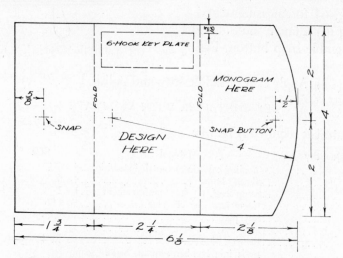

Fig. 73. Working Drawing for Key Container with Key Plate

Order of procedure:

(1) Draw and cut out the pattern. See Fig. 73 for dimensions.

(2) Place pattern on smooth side of leather and mark around with sharp pencil or awl.

(3) Remove pattern and cut out leather on the outline with sharp scissors, Fig. 25.

(4) Mark size of cut-out leather on durable tracing paper.

(5) Select or create appropriate design. See section on Designs, at the back of the book.

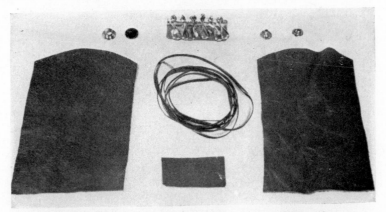

Fig. 74. Material Required for Key Container with Key Plate

(6) Trace or draw design on paper, Fig. 26.

(7) Moisten reverse side of leather for tooling, Fig. 27.

(8) Transfer design to leather, Fig. 28.

(9) Remove tracing paper and press pattern lines into leather, Fig. 29.

(10) Decorate the design with deerfoot modeler, Figs. 44 and 45, or by stippling, Fig. 62.

(11) Mark location for key-plate eyelets on skived lining.

(12) Punch holes for key plate with eyelet punch, Fig. 75.

(13) Locate and punch similar holes on small reinforcement piece.

(14) Cement reinforcement piece in its respective position on lining.

(15) Insert eyelets through key plate, lining, and reinforcement piece, Fig. 76, and fasten securely with eyelet-setting punch. The reinforcement piece serves to strengthen the lining.

(16) Apply rubber cement to inner edges of both cover and lining material, Fig. 32.

(17) Press the cemented pieces together firmly, Fig. 33. Because the lining has less space to bend in than the cover piece, it will be necessary to fold the material as the pieces are

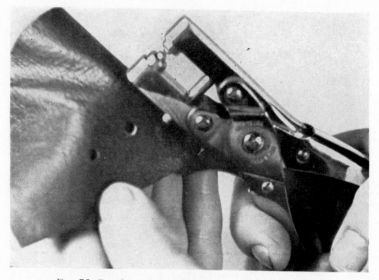

Fig. 75. Punching Eyelet Holes for Fastening Key Plate

Fig. 76. Fastening Key Plate to Lining

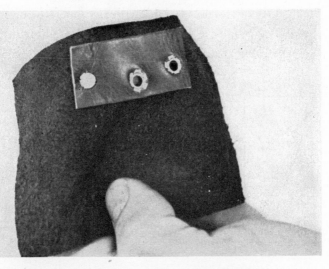

Fig. 77. Position of Reinforcement on Lining

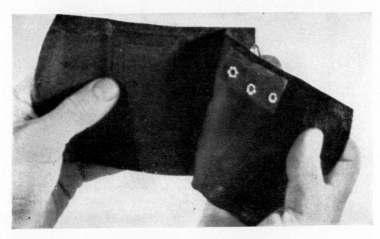

Fig. 78. Pressing Lining to Cover

being pressed together. This will distribute the pull so that the lining will not wrinkle or buckle at the folds.

CORNER LACING

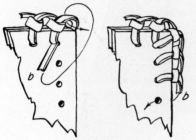

Fig. 79. Detail of Corner with Buttonhole Stitch

(18) Trim irregularities from material, Fig. 34.

(19) Color the edges with India ink, Fig. 35.

(20) Punch the edges for lacing with lacing gauge punch, Fig. 36.

(21) Lace the edge either with the whip stitch, Fig. 37, or with buttonhole stitch, Figs. 46–49. A 90-

SPLICING EDGE LACING

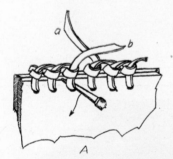

Fig. 80. Detail of Lace Ending or Fastening

degree corner hole should be entered twice to make a square corner, Fig. 79.

(22) Complete the lacing process with a splice, Fig. 80:

(a) Pry or work end *b* out of its loop, Fig. 80–A.

(b) Insert end *a* through the loop just opened, Fig. 80–B.

(c) Pull end *b* through the lace hole of the first thickness of leather and drop it between the two layers.

(d) Insert end *a* into this hole left open by *b*, Fig. 80–C, and drop it between the two layers with *b*. Place a drop of rubber cement between the lining and the cover where ends *a* and *b* are placed. This makes them fast and it should be impossible to detect this type of splice if properly executed.

(23) Roll the laced edges with a mallet, Fig. 52.

(24) Mark, punch holes, and assemble snap-button assembly, Figs. 54–58.

(25) Apply coat of saddle soap and polish, Figs. 38 and 39.

3.

Coin Purses

T HE COIN PURSES presented in this section are easy to make and sufficiently well designed to be ornamental as well as useful. They are ideal projects for girls, because they appeal to the creative side of their character as well as being presentable as gifts.

Fig. 81. A Group of Coin Purses

Fig. 82. Coin Purse, Closed and Open

The combination coin-purse key-container not only serves a dual purpose in its use, but involves a few of the more advanced operations.

The designs are so planned that a monogram may be placed and tooled on the project to personalize it. The purses also are very attractive when made from some of the nontooling leathers, such as alligator.

COIN PURSE WITH SNAP BUTTON

Materials required (Fig. 84):

Quantity	Material	Size
1	Tooling calfskin or mottled steerhide A	4 x 7
1	Tooling calfskin or mottled steerhide B	3¼ x 4
1	Edge lace—bevel edge	3⁄32 x 96
1	Snap-button assembly	3⁄8
	India ink	
	Rubber cement	
	Saddle soap	

Essential tools (Fig. 12):

cement applier (15), dye brush (18), edge creaser (10), lacing gauge punch (1), mallet (13), paper clips, pencil (6), scissors (2), sheepskin polisher (14), snap-setting outfit (22), sponge, tracer and deerfoot modeler (9), and waxing cloth.

Order of procedure:

(1) Draw and cut out the pattern. See Fig. 83 for measurements.

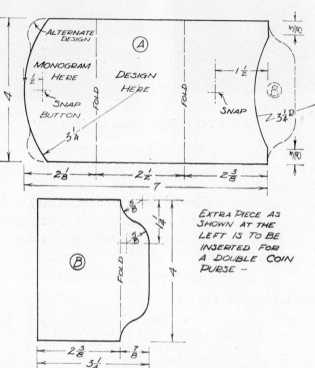

Fig. 83. Working Drawing of Coin Purse with Snap Button

(2) Place pattern on smooth side of leather and mark around with sharp pencil or awl.

(3) Remove pattern and cut out leather on the outline with sharp scissors, Fig. 25.

(4) Mark size of cut-out leather on durable tracing paper.

(5) Select or create appropriate design. See section on Designs, at back of book.

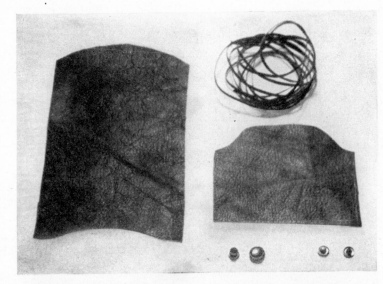

Fig. 84. Material Required for Coin Purse with Snap Button

(6) Trace or draw design on paper, Fig. 26.

(7) Moisten reverse or rough side of leather, Fig. 27.

(8) Transfer design to leather, Fig. 28.

(9) Remove tracing paper and press pattern lines into leather, Fig. 29.

(10) Decorate the design with deerfoot modeler, Figs. 44 and 45, or by stippling, Fig. 62.

(11) Skive the inside edges of those portions of piece A which are to be folded together, Fig. 31.

(12) Skive the inside edges of piece B if the project is to be a double coin purse.

(13) Apply rubber cement along the skived edges which are to be fastened together, Fig. 32.

(14) Press the rough side of piece B firmly to the rough side of piece A to form the first pocket, Fig. 85.

(15) Apply cement to the edges of the flesh side of piece B, Fig. 32.

Fig. 85. Forming First Pocket of Coin Purse

Fig. 86. Forming Second Pocket of Coin Purse

(16) Press the newly cemented edges firmly to form the second pocket, Fig. 86.

(17) Trim irregularities from purse edges, Fig. 34.

(18) Color edges with India ink, Fig. 35.

(19) Punch edges for lacing with lacing gauge punch, Fig. 36.

(20) Lace the edge with the whip stitch, Fig. 37, or with buttonhole stitch, Figs. 46–49 and 79.

(21) Roll edges with mallet, Fig. 52.

(22) Mark, punch holes, and assemble snap-button assembly, Figs. 54–58.

(23) Crease edges not laced or folded, Fig. 68.

(24) Apply coat of saddle soap and polish, Figs. 38 and 39.

ZIPPER COIN-PURSE KEY-CASE

Material required (Fig. 90):

Quantity	Material	Size
1	Tooling calfskin or mottled steerhide A	4 x 5¼
1	Tooling calfskin or mottled steerhide C	3½ x 4¾
1	Tooling calfskin or mottled steerhide D	2 x 3½
1	Skiver lining B	4 x 5⅛
1	Edge lace—bevel edge	³⁄₃₂ x 108
1	Zipper	7 inch
1	Key plate	6-hook
3	Eyelets	To fit key plate
	Thread—mercerized, color of leather	No. 40
2	Goatskin-thong lace—contrasting color	³⁄₃₂ x 10
	India ink	
	Rubber cement	
	Saddle soap	

Essential tools (Fig. 12):

cement applier (15), dye brush (18), edge creaser (10), eyelet-setting punch (4), lacing gauge punch (1), mallet (13), paper clips, pencil (6), scissors (2), sewing machine, sheepskin polisher (14), sponge, thong-rolling block, tracer and deerfoot modeler (9), and waxing cloth.

Order of Procedure:

(1) Draw and cut out patterns. See Fig. 89 for dimensions.

Fig. 87. Zipper Coin Purse, Closed

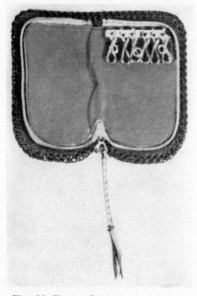

Fig. 88. Zipper Coin Purse, Opened

(2) Place patterns on smooth side of leather and mark around with sharp pencil or awl.

(3) Remove pattern and cut out leather on the outline with sharp scissors, Fig. 25.

(4) Mark size of cover A on durable tracing paper.

(5) Select or create design for tooling. See section on Designs.

(6) Trace or draw design on tracing paper, Fig. 26.

(7) Moisten reverse side of cover A, Fig. 27.

(8) Transfer design to cover A, Fig. 28.

(9) Remove tracing paper and press pattern lines into leather, Fig. 29.

(10) Decorate the design with deerfoot modeler, Fig. 44 and 45 or by stippling, Fig. 62.

(11) Skive the inside edges of pocket D, Fig. 31.

(12) Apply rubber cement along the skived edges of pocket D and on the edges of the flesh side of cover C, Fig. 32.

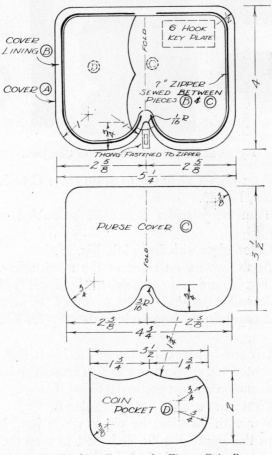

Fig. 89. Working Drawing for Zipper Coin Purse

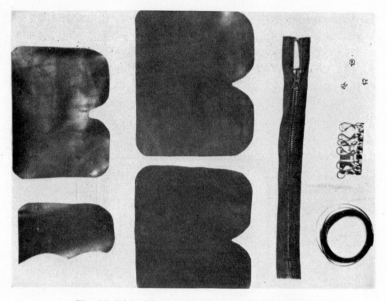

Fig. 90. Materials Required for Zipper Coin Purse

(13) Press pocket D firmly to purse cover C to form the coin pocket, Fig. 33.

(14) Trim irregularities from the assembled material, Fig. 34.

(15) Color edges with India ink, Fig. 35.

(16) Apply cement on edges of the rough side of purse cover C, Fig. 32, and to the face side of the zipper cloth.

(17) Assemble the zipper to purse cover C by pressing the cemented edges firmly. See working drawing for location of zipper.

(18) Lay purse cover C on lining B to locate that portion to be cemented and apply narrow strip of cement on back edge of purse C and on marked portion of lining B.

(19) Press purse cover C firmly to lining B.

(20) Sew with machine the pieces which have been cemented to the zipper, Fig. 91. It is best to keep the line of sewing approximately ⅛ inch from the outer edge of purse.

(21) Mark locations, punch, and fasten key plate in position, Figs. 75 and 76.

(22) Apply rubber cement along inside edges of lining *B* and on edges of rough side of cover *A*.

(23) Press the cemented pieces together firmly.

(24) Trim irregularities from the edges, Fig. 34.

(25) Color edges with India ink, Fig. 35.

(26) Punch edges for lacing with a lacing gauge punch, Fig. 36.

(27) Lace the edges with whip stitch, Fig. 37 or with buttonhole stitch, Figs. 46–49, 79, and 80.

(28) Roll edges with mallet, Fig. 52.

(29) Apply coat of saddle soap and polish, Figs. 38 and 39.

(30) OPTIONAL: Make the thong on the zipper end for convenient opening and closing for key-case coin-purse if desired. See p. 164.

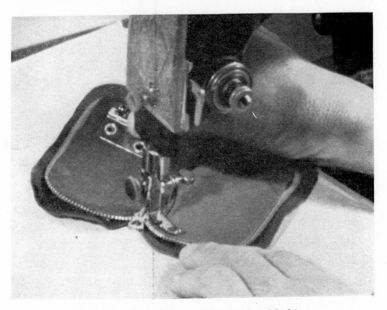

Fig. 91. Sewing Zipper in Place with a Machine

4.

Wristbands

THE WRISTBANDS pictured in Fig. 92 are of two types, coin purse and wrist-watch band. The coin purse is definitely a girl's type but involves many of the operations of the wrist-watch band.

The making of either project is quite simple, yet new operations are presented. The wrist-watch band is possibly one of

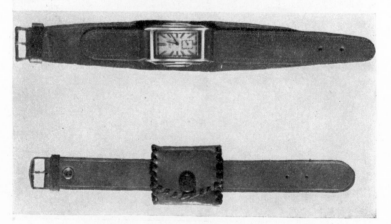

Fig. 92. Two Types of Wristbands

98

the most useful projects and will prove to be among the most popular.

Designs may be tooled or stamped to suit the individuality of the craftsman.

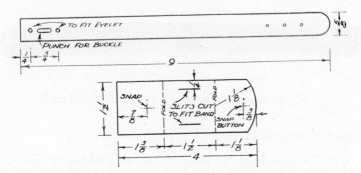

Fig. 93. Working Drawing of Wristband Coin Purse

WRISTBAND COIN PURSE

Materials required (Fig. 94):

Quantity	Material	Size
1	Tooling calfskin	⅝ x 9
1	Tooling calfskin	1½ x 4
1	Edge lace—bevel edge	³⁄₃₂ x 30
1	Wristband buckle	⅝
1	Snap-button assembly	⅜
1	Eyelet	
	India ink	
	Rubber cement	
	Saddle soap	

Essential tools (Fig. 12):

cement applier (15), dye brush (18), edge creaser (10), eyelet setting punch (4), lacing gauge punch (1), mallet (13), scissors (2), sheepskin polisher (14), skiving knife (7), snap-setting outfit (22), and waxing cloth.

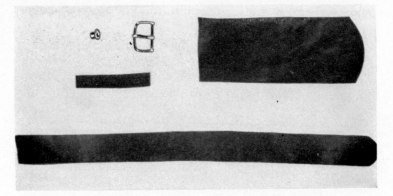

Fig. 94. Materials Required for Wristband Coin Purse

Order of procedure:

(1) Draw and cut out the pattern. See working drawing for dimensions.

(2) Place patterns on smooth side of leather and mark around with sharp pencil or awl.

(3) Mark coin purse for slits. See working drawing for measurements.

(4) Cut the slits with sharp knife, Fig. 67.

(5) Skive inside edges which are to be cemented together for making pocket of purse, Fig. 31.

(6) Apply rubber cement along skived edges, Fig. 32.

(7) Fold purse and press cemented edges firmly to make pocket.

(8) Trim irregularities from edges, Fig. 34.

(9) Color edges with India ink, Fig. 35.

(10) Punch edges of coin purse for lacing, Fig. 36. The folded edge need not be punched.

(11) Lace the edges with the simple whip stitch, Fig. 37.

(12) Mark, punch, and assemble snap buttons, Figs. 54–58.

(13) Punch holes, as indicated in Fig. 93 for the buckle.

(14) Crease edges not laced or folded, Fig. 68.

(15) Insert wristband buckle and fasten with eyelet.

(16) Apply coat of saddle soap and polish both pieces, Figs. 38 and 39.

(17) Insert the wristband through the slits of the purse.

(18) Punch two or three buckle holes for the correct adjustment of the wristband to the wrist.

WRIST-WATCH BAND

Materials required (Fig. 96):

Quantity	Material	Size
1	Tooling calfskin A	1⅛ x 9½
1	Tooling calfskin B	½ x 4½
1	Tooling calfskin C	½ x 2
1	Tooling calfskin—loop	¼ x 1¾
1	Wristband buckle	¾
	Thread—mercerized	No. 40
	India ink	
	Rubber cement	
	Saddle soap	

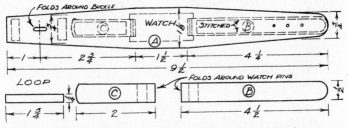

Fig. 95. Working Drawing for Wrist-Watch Band

Essential tools (Fig. 12):

cement applier (15), dye brush (18), edge creaser (10), lacing gauge punch (1), scissors (2), sewing machine, sheepskin polisher (14), skiving knife (7), and waxing cloth.

Order of procedure:

(1) Draw and cut out the patterns. See Fig. 95 for dimensions.

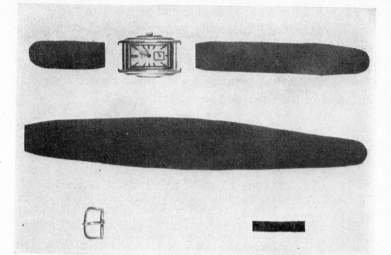

Fig. 96. Materials Required for Wrist-Watch Band

(2) Place patterns on smooth side of leather and mark around with sharp pencil or awl.

(3) Color the edges of all parts with India ink, Fig. 35.

(4) Crease the edges of piece A with an edge creaser, Fig. 68.

(5) Skive the ends of pieces B and C, which are to be folded around the assembly pins of the wrist watch, Fig. 31.

(6) Apply rubber cement along the skived ends, Fig. 32.

(7) Fasten pieces B and C around the pins of the watch by folding and pressing the cemented ends firmly for stitching.

(8) Sew pieces B and C, respectively, for holding pins.

(9) Locate position of pieces B and C on band A. To do this accurately, the pieces should be attached to the watch.

(10) Apply rubber cement to the back sides of B and C and to the face side of A where the pieces are to be attached, Fig. 32. See Fig. 95 for proper location.

(11) Remove the watch and stitch pieces B and C to A as indicated in Fig. 95. Refer to Fig. 91 for sewing.

(12) Punch holes for the buckle.

(13) Skive ends of loop piece.

(14) Apply rubber cement to skived ends of loop, Fig. 32.

(15) Fold loop around buckle end of band to determine correct size of loop, and press the cemented ends firmly together.

(16) Skive back side of buckle end of band.

(17) Apply rubber cement on skived end of band.

(18) Slip the loop over the buckle end, insert buckle, and press cemented portion in the proper place for sewing.

(19) Sew buckle and loop in respective places. See Fig. 91 for sewing and Fig. 95 for proper line of sewing.

(20) Apply coat of saddle soap and polish the band with sheepskin polisher.

(21) Assemble watch in the wristband and punch two or three holes for the correct adjustment of the band to the wrist.

5.

Cigarette Case

THE PROJECT shown in Fig. 97 is but one of the many types of cigarette cases that may be made. This particular one has proved popular because it holds both cigarettes and matches and because when buttoned the flap will stay secure.

The variety of operations involved in the making of this case holds the interest of the craftsman. The process of stretching the case to assure proper fit for the pack is one that should not be overlooked. Once stretched, the case will keep its form permanently.

CIGARETTE CASE

Materials required (Fig. 100):

Quantity	Material	Size
1	Tooling calfskin or mottled steerhide A	3½ x 7½
1	Tooling calfskin or mottled steerhide B	3⅜ x 3½
1	Tooling calfskin or mottled steerhide C	1½ x 2
1	Edge lace—bevel edge	³⁄₃₂ x 84
1	Snap-button assembly	⅜
	Thread—mercerized	No. 40
	India ink	
	Rubber cement	
	Saddle soap	

Essential tools (Fig. 12):

cement applier (15), dye brush (18), edge creaser (10), lacing gauge punch (1), mallet (13), paper clips, scissors (2), sewing machine, sheepskin polisher (14), snap-setting outfit (22), skiving knife (7), sponge, stretching block, tracer and deerfoot modeler (9), and waxing cloth.

Order of procedure:

(1) Draw and cut out the patterns. See Fig. 99 for measurements.

(2) Place patterns on smooth side of leather and mark around with sharp pencil or awl.

(3) Remove patterns and cut out leather on the outline with sharp scissors, Fig. 25.

Fig. 97. Cigarette Case, Closed

(4) Mark size of cover piece A on durable tracing paper.

(5) Select or create appropriate design. See section on Designs, at back of book.

Fig. 98. Cigarette Case, Open

(6) Trace or draw design on paper, Fig. 26.

(7) Moisten reverse or rough side of cover piece A.

(8) Transfer design to leather, Fig. 28.

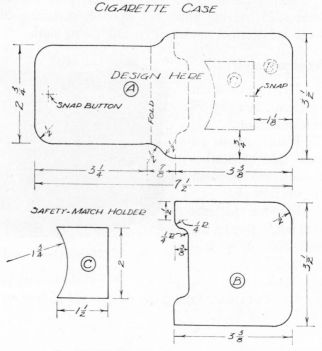

Fig. 99. Working Drawing of Cigarette Case

(9) Remove tracing paper and press pattern lines into leather, Fig. 29.

(10) Decorate the design with deerfoot modeler, Figs. 44 and 45, or by stippling, Fig. 62.

(11) Skive inside edges of piece C, Fig. 31.

(12) Color edges of piece C with India ink, Fig. 35.

(13) Apply rubber cement, Fig. 32, on skived edge of piece C and on the face side of piece B, where C is to be located.

(14) Press match holder C firmly to piece B.

Fig. 100. Materials Required for Cigarette Case

(15) Sew C to piece B, Fig. 91.

(16) Skive inside edges of pieces A and B where they are to be fastened.

(17) Apply rubber cement on skived edges of pieces A and B.

(18) Press B firmly to cover A to form pocket.

(19) Trim irregularities along edge, Fig. 34.

(20) Color edges with India ink, Fig. 35.

(21) Punch edges for lacing, Fig. 36.

(22) Lace the edges with the buttonhole stitch, Figs. 46–49 and 79 or with the whip stitch, Fig. 37. Start lacing on bottom so splice can be easily made.

(23) Roll the laced edges, Fig. 52.

(24) Mark, punch, and assemble the snap-button assembly, Figs. 54–58.

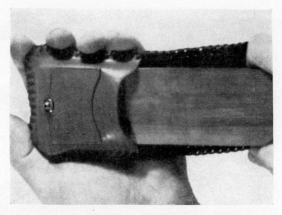

Fig. 101. Stretching the Case to Fit Packet

(25) Crease the top edges of pieces *B* and *C* with an edge creaser, Fig. 68.

(26) Moisten the inside of the large pocket slightly and stretch the case with a block the same size as a cigarette pack, Fig. 101. Edges of block should be rounded so leather will not be cut.

(27) After project has dried thoroughly, apply coat of saddle soap and polish, Figs. 38 and 39.

6.

Billfolds

Fig. 102 shows open and closed views of the billfolds described and illustrated. Although these projects have been arranged in the order of their difficulty, the first billfold has proved to be the most popular.

The tooling designs in the Design section are so flexible that any initial or monogram may be suitably arranged either on the design itself or on that portion of the billfold not decorated.

Fig. 102. Billfolds

109

The second and third billfolds involve sewing by machine and are rather difficult to sew unless one practices with the machine prior to this operation. However, if care is exercised, the craftsman need have no hesitancy about making any of these billfolds.

The double-fold billfold is a very elaborate one which has a retail cost many times that which the novice need pay for the material.

SINGLE-FOLD BILLFOLD

Materials required (Fig. 105):

Quantity	Material	Size
1	Tooling calfskin or mottled steerhide A	3½ x 8½
1	Tooling calfskin or mottled steerhide B	3¼ x 8⅜
1	Tooling calfskin or mottled steerhide C	3¼ x 3¾
1	Tooling calfskin or mottled steerhide D	2½ x 3¼
1	Edge lace—bevel edge	³⁄₃₂ x 104
	India ink	
	Rubber cement	
	Saddle soap	

Essential tools (Fig. 12):

cement applier (15), dye brush (18), edge creaser (10), lacing gauge punch (1), mallet (13), paper clips, scissors (2), sheepskin polisher (14), skiving knife (7), sponge, tracer and deerfoot modeler (9), and waxing cloth.

Order of procedure:

(1) Draw and cut out the patterns. See Fig. 104 for measurements.

(2) Place patterns on smooth side of leather and mark around with sharp pencil or awl.

(3) Remove patterns and cut out leather pieces on outline with sharp scissors, Fig. 25.

(4) Mark size of cover piece A on durable tracing paper.

(5) Select or create appropriate design. See section on Designs.

(6) Trace or draw design on paper, Fig. 26.

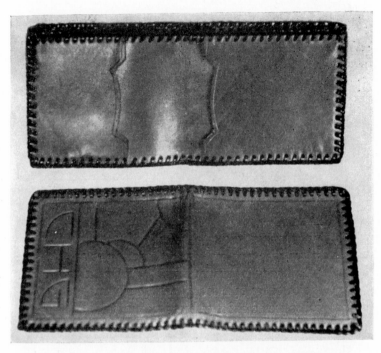

Fig. 103. Single-Fold Billfold

(7) Moisten reverse or rough side of A, Fig. 27.

(8) Transfer design to leather, Fig. 28.

(9) Remove tracing paper and press pattern lines into leather, Fig. 29.

(10) Decorate the design with deerfoot modeler, Figs. 44 and 45, or by stippling, Fig. 62.

(11) Skive inside edges of pockets C and D, Fig. 31.

(12) Color the open edges of C and D with India ink, Fig. 35.

(13) Crease open-end edges of C and D with edge creaser, Fig. 68.

(14) Skive the edges, Fig. 31, of face side of B, to which C and D will be cemented.

BILL FOLD

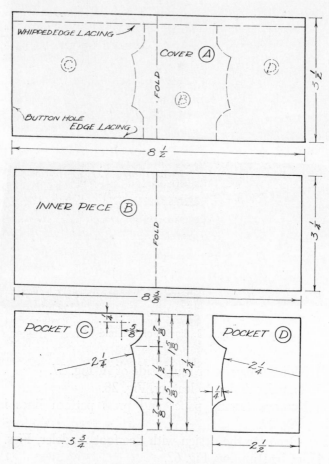

Fig. 104. Working Drawing for Simple Billfold

Fig. 105. Materials Required for Single-Fold Billfold

(15) Apply rubber cement on skived edges of pieces B, C, and D, Fig. 32.

(16) Press C and D firmly to inner piece B, thus forming the two pockets.

(17) Trim irregularities from edges thus far assembled, Fig. 34.

(18) Color edges with India ink, Fig. 35.

(19) Punch top edge for lacing, Fig. 36.

(20) Lace with simple whip stitch, Fig. 37.

(21) Skive inside edges of cover A. Skive only that portion of the two ends and bottom to which inner piece B is to be cemented.

(22) Apply rubber cement on skived edges of cover A and on back edges of both ends and bottom of inner piece B.

(23) Press both parts together firmly. The inner piece is slightly shorter than the cover so that the billfold will close without wrinkling.

(24) Trim irregularities from assembled edges.

(25) Color edges of project.

(26) Punch the edges for lacing.

(27) Lace edges with buttonhole stitch, Figs. 46–49 and 79. Start lace at bottom so splicing will work out.

(28) Roll laced edges, Fig. 52.

. (29) Apply coat of saddle soap and polish, Figs. 38 and 39.

Fig. 106. Single-Fold Billfold with Flap

SINGLE-FOLD BILLFOLD WITH FLAP

Materials required (Fig. 108):

Quantity	Material	Size
1	Tooling calfskin or mottled steerhide A	3¼ x 14½
1	Tooling calfskin or mottled steerhide B	3 x 8⅜
1	Tooling calfskin or mottled steerhide C	3 x 5¾
1	Tooling calfskin or mottled steerhide D	⅝ x 1½
1	Edge lace—bevel edge	3/32 x 84
	Thread—mercerized	No. 40
	India ink	
	Rubber cement	
	Saddle soap	

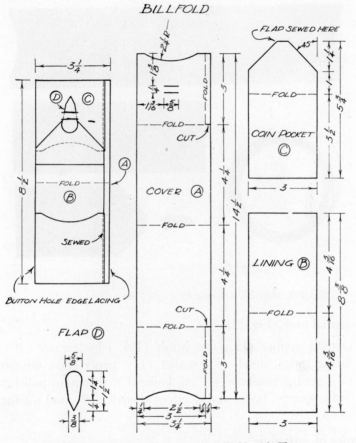

Fig. 107. Working Drawing for Billfold with Flap

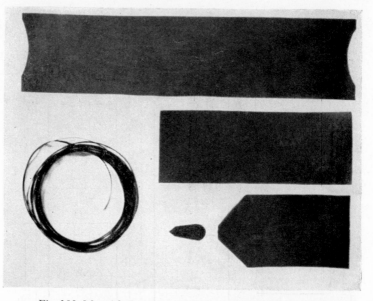

Fig. 108. Materials Required for Single-Fold Billfold with Flap

Essential tools (Fig. 12):

cement applier (15), dye brush (18), edge creaser (10), lacing gauge punch (1), mallet (13), paper clips, scissors (2), sewing machine, skiving knife (7), sheepskin polisher (14), sponge, tracer and deerfoot modeler (9), and waxing cloth.

Order of procedure:

(1) Draw and cut out the patterns. See Fig. 107 for measurements.

(2) Place patterns on smooth side of leather and mark around with sharp pencil or awl.

(3) Remove patterns and cut out leather pieces on outline with sharp scissors, Fig. 25.

(4) Mark size of cover piece A on durable tracing paper.

(5) Select or create appropriate design. See section on Designs, at back of book.

(6) Trace or draw design on paper, Fig. 26.

(7) Moisten reverse or rough side of A, Fig. 27.

(8) Transfer design to leather, Fig. 28.

(9) Remove tracing paper and press pattern lines into leather, Fig. 29.

(10) Decorate the design with deerfoot modeler, Figs. 44 and 45.

(11) Cut flap slits as indicated in drawing.

(12) Cut the short, side slits at both ends of piece A.

(13) Fold narrow edge strips at both ends of A. Moisten at the fold and the shape will be retained.

(14) Fold two ends toward center on A, for pockets.

(15) Cement and sew flap D on pocket C.

(16) Cement and sew pocket C to lining B.

(17) Apply rubber cement on the unfinished edges of the two narrow edge folds on piece A; also apply cement to the edge of lining B that is to be sewed.

(18) Press cemented edges of A firmly to lining B. This forms the two coin purses and bill container.

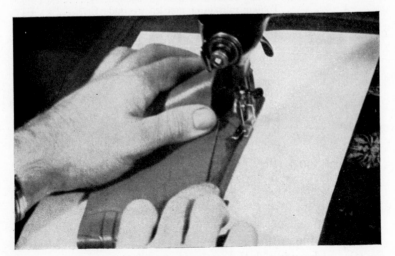

Fig. 109. Sewing Billfold with Machine

(19) Sew narrow folds to lining B. Use piece of paper between leather and machine feeder to prevent leather from being injured.

(20) Skive bottom inside edges of billfold, Fig. 31.

(21) Apply rubber cement on skived edges, Fig. 32.

(22) Press cemented edges firmly together.

(23) Trim irregularities from project for even edge, Fig. 34.

(24) Color edges with India ink, Fig. 35.

(25) Crease all edges which are not to be laced or folded, Fig. 68.

(26) Punch top and bottom edges with lacing gauge punch.

(27) Lace the two edges with buttonhole stitch, Figs. 46–49.

(28) Roll the laced edges with mallet, Fig. 52.

(29) Apply coat of saddle soap and polish, Figs. 38 and 39.

DOUBLE-FOLD BILLFOLD

Materials required (Fig. 112):

Quantity	Material	Size
1	Tooling calfskin or mottled steerhide A	4¾ x 8½
1	Tooling calfskin or mottled steerhide C	2⅜ x 4½
1	Tooling calfskin or mottled steerhide D	2 x 3¾
1	Tooling calfskin or mottled steerhide E	2½ x 4½
1	Tooling calfskin or mottled steerhide F	2⅝ x 4½
1	Skiver lining B	4½ x 8⅜
1	Edge lace—bevel edge	³⁄₃₂ x 120
1	Isinglass	2¼ x 4¼
	Thread—mercerized	No. 40
1	Snap-button assembly	
	India ink	
	Rubber cement	
	Saddle soap	

Essential tools (Fig. 12):

cement applier (15), dye brush (18), edge creaser (10), lacing gauge punch (1), mallet (13), paper clips, scissors (2), sewing machine, skiving knife (7), sheepskin polisher (14), snap-setting outfit (22), sponge, tracer and deerfoot modeler (9), and waxing cloth.

Fig. 110. Double-Fold Billfold

Order of procedure:

(1) Draw and cut out the patterns. See Fig. 111 for measurements.

(2) Place patterns on smooth side of leather and mark around with sharp pencil or awl.

(3) Remove patterns and cut out pieces with scissors, Fig. 25.

(4) Mark size of cover piece A on durable tracing paper.

(5) Select or create appropriate design. See section on Designs, at back of book.

(6) Trace or draw design on paper.

(7) Moisten reverse or rough side of A, Fig. 27.

(8) Transfer design to leather, Fig. 28.

(9) Remove tracing paper and press pattern lines into leather, Fig. 29.

(10) Decorate design, Figs. 44 and 45.

(11) Apply rubber cement to unfinished side of E.

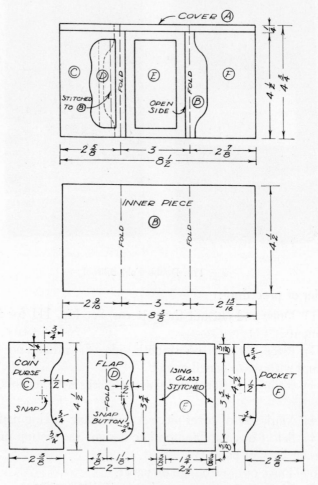

Fig. 111. Working Drawing for Double-Fold Billfold

(12) Press E firmly to isinglass.

(13) Stitch isinglass to E.

(14) Apply rubber cement to that portion of D which is to

Fig. 112. Materials required for Double-Fold Billfold

be fastened to inner piece B.

(15) Press flap D firmly in proper position on inner piece B.

(16) Sew piece D to piece B.

(17) Skive edges which are to be fastened to B, of purse C and pocket F, on the rough side.

(18) Apply rubber cement to skived edges of C, F, the top and bottom edges of E, and on the finished edges of inner piece B.

(19) Press pieces C, E, and F on respective places on B.

(20) Stitch C, E, and F, on

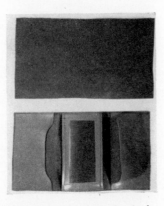

Fig. 113. Inner Parts Ready for Assembly to Cover

three edges to B. This permits opening of purse C and pocket F and leaves one side of E open for insertion of identification cards, etc. Fig. 113.

(21) Mark location, punch holes, and assemble snap button on pocket. Figs. 54–58.

(22) Skive bottom and two ends on back side of A.

(23) Apply rubber cement to skived edges of A and to corresponding edges of B.

(24) Press the two pieces firmly together.

(25) Trim irregularities from edges.

(26) Color edges with India ink.

(27) Crease all edges which are not laced or folded.

(28) Punch edges for lacing, Fig. 36.

(29) Lace the edges with buttonhole stitch, Figs. 46–49, 79 and 80.

(30) Roll the laced edges with mallet, Fig. 52.

(31) Apply coat of saddle soap and polish, Figs. 38 and 39.

7

Ladies' Zipper Handbag

THE LADIES' HANDBAG here discussed has many possibilities, such as are shown in Fig. 114. The upper purse in this figure

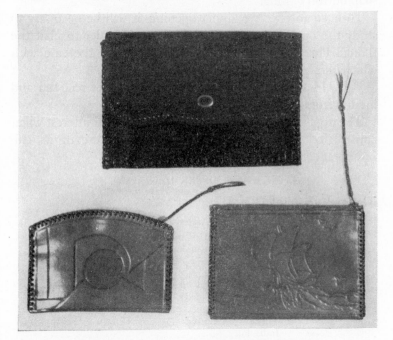

Fig. 114. Group of Ladies' Handbags

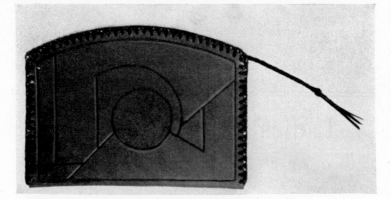

Fig. 115. Ladies' Zipper Handbag

might easily be considered an underarm bag because of its snap-button closing.

To have an effective zipper opening, it will be necessary to study the operations in making a thong in order to plait the thong. This type of pull adds appreciably to the ease with which the bag may be opened and closed.

Fig. 115 shows the handbag with the zipper recessed and hidden from view.

The upper handbag in Fig. 114 takes on added interest when constructed from alligator skin, which, because of its embossed effect, needs no tooling.

LADIES' ZIPPER HANDBAG

Materials required (Fig. 117):

Quantity	Material	Size
1	Tooling calfskin or mottled steerhide A	7 x 9
2	Tooling calfskin or mottled steerhide C	1 x 7¼
1	Skiver lining B	7 x 8½
1	Zipper	7 inches
1	Edge lace—bevel edge	3/32 x 84
2	Edge lace (optional), contrasting colors for thong zipper pull	3/32 x 10
	Thread—mercerized	No. 40
	India ink	
	Rubber cement	
	Saddle soap	

Essential tools (Fig. 12):

cement applier (*15*), dye brush (*18*), lacing gauge punch (*1*), mallet (*13*), paper clips, scissors (*2*), sewing machine, sheepskin polisher (*14*), skiving knife (*7*), sponge, tracer and deerfoot modeler (*9*), and waxing cloth.

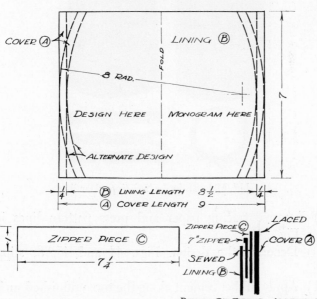

Fig. 116. Working Drawing for Ladies' Zipper Handbag

Order of procedure:

(1) Draw and cut out the patterns. See Fig. 116 for measurements.

(2) Place patterns on smooth side of leather and mark around with sharp pencil.

(3) Remove patterns and cut out leather pieces on outline with sharp scissors, Fig. 25.

(4) Mark size of cover A on durable tracing paper.

(5) Select or create appropriate design. See section on Designs, at back of book.

(6) Trace or draw design on paper.

(7) Moisten reverse or rough side of A, Fig. 27.

(8) Transfer design to leather, Fig. 28.

Fig. 117. Materials for Ladies' Zipper Handbag

(9) Remove tracing paper and press pattern lines into leather, Fig. 29.

(10) Decorate the design, Figs. 44 and 45, or stipple, Fig. 62.

(11) Apply rubber cement along the top, unfinished surface of B and to one side of the zipper tape. See that the zipper will open correctly.

(12) Press cemented edges firmly together.

(13) Apply rubber cement to other surface of zipper tape and to one edge of finished surface of narrow piece C.

(14) Press cemented pieces firmly together. See working drawing.

(15) Sew zipper to lining B and to zipper piece C.

(16) Cement and sew other half of zipper.

(17) Skive inside edges of cover A.

(18) Apply rubber cement along outside edges of rough surface of lining B, on rough surface of attached piece C, and also on skived edges of cover A.

(19) Press cemented parts firmly together.

(20) Trim irregularities from project edges, Fig. 34.

(21) Color edges with India ink, Fig. 35.

(22) Punch edges for lacing, Fig. 36.

(23) Lace one top edge first with buttonhole stitch, Figs. 46–49, and then the other edges. Start lacing on bottom edge for splicing, Figs. 79 and 80.

(24) Roll laced edges with mallet, Fig. 52.

(25) Clean with saddle soap and polish, Figs. 38 and 39.

(26) Make thong for zipper, if desired. See p. 164.

8.

Desk Accessories

$\mathbf{T}$HE LETTER HOLDER in Fig. 118 and the book ends in Fig. 123 are somewhat similar in construction in that they use a

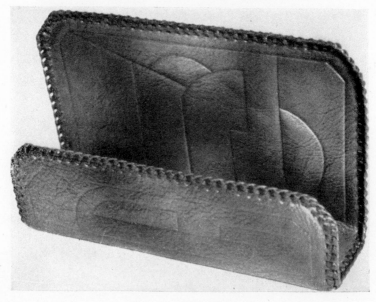

Fig. 118. Letter Holder

metal form around which the leather is laced. Both projects are a necessity as well as a decoration for desks, the need for either being obvious.

Since both are larger-type projects, steerhide with a mottled color effect creates a very interesting surface design, and makes tooling optional. The basic operations for these projects are a repetition of those carried out in earlier ones; however, a high degree of skill is essential to develop interesting and well-executed projects.

The book end involves decidedly new operations in raising certain parts of the design, called "repousse" modeling; and in padding the metal form with a sheet of cotton to give an upholstered appearance. This adds greatly to the attractiveness and value of the project.

LETTER HOLDER

Materials required (Fig. 120):

Quantity	Material	Size
1	Tooling calfskin or mottled steerhide	7⅜ x 8½
1	Tooling calfskin or mottled steerhide	7⅜ x 8⅛
1	Sheet-metal form—18 or 20 gauge	6⅞ x 8
1	Edge lace—bevel edges	³⁄₃₂ x 120
	India ink; Rubber cement; Saddle soap	

Essential tools (Fig. 12):

cement applier (15), dye brush (18), lacing gauge punch (1), mallet (13), paper clips, scissors (2), skiving knife (7), sheepskin polisher (14), sponge, tracer and deerfoot modeler (9), and waxing cloth.

Order of procedure:

(1) Draw and cut out patterns. See working drawing for measurements.

(2) Place patterns on smooth side of leather and mark around with sharp pencil.

(3) Remove patterns and cut out leather pieces on outline with sharp scissors, Fig. 25.

(4) Mark size of design area on durable tracing paper.

(5) Select or create appropriate design. See section on Designs at back of book.

(6) Trace or draw design on paper.

(7) Moisten the unfinished or rough side of both pieces, Fig. 27. Moisten only those portions on which a design is to be tooled.

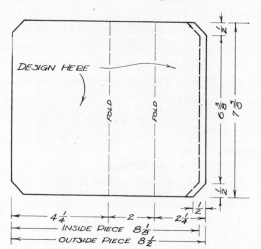

LETTER HOLDER

Fig. 119. Working Drawing for Letter Holder

(8) Transfer design to both pieces of leather, Fig. 28.

(9) Remove tracing paper and press pattern lines firmly into leather, Fig. 29.

(10) Decorate the design, Figs. 44 and 45.

(11) Skive inside edges of both pieces, Fig. 31.

(12) Apply rubber cement to skived edges, Fig. 32.

(13) Place metal form in its proper position on the outside piece of leather, and then place the inside piece in its relative position, Fig. 121.

(14) Press cemented edges together to conform with the bends of the metal form, Fig. 121.

(15) Trim irregularities of assembled pieces. Allow approximately 3/16 inch of leather beyond form for lacing, Fig. 122.

(16) Color edges with India ink, Fig. 35.

(17) Punch edges for lacing, Fig. 36.

(18) Lace edges with buttonhole stitch, Figs. 46–49 and 79.

(19) Roll the laced edges with a mallet, Fig. 52.

(20) Clean with saddle soap and polish, Figs. 38 and 39.

Fig. 120. Materials for Letter Holder

Fig. 121. Pressing Leather Around Metal Form

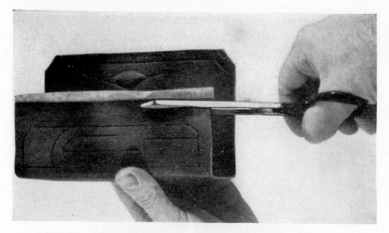

Fig. 122. Trimming Irregularities from Edges of Letter Holder

BOOK END

Materials required (Fig. 125):

Quantity	Material	Size
1	Tooling calfskin or mottled steerhide	5¾ x 9½
1	Tooling calfskin or mottled steerhide	5¾ x 9¼
1	Sheet-metal form—18 or 20 gauge	5¼ x 9
1	Edge lace—bevel edge	⅜₂ x 120
1	Cotton—thin sheet	6 x 10
	India ink	
	Rubber cement	
	Saddle soap	

Essential tools (Fig. 12):

cement applier (*15*), dye brush (*18*), lacing gauge punch (*1*), mallet (*13*), paper clips, scissors (*2*), skiving knife (*7*), sheepskin polisher (*14*), sponge, tracer and spoon modeler (*8*), and waxing cloth.

Order of procedure:

(1) Draw and cut out patterns. See Fig. 124 for measurements.

(2) Place patterns on smooth side of leather and mark around with sharp pencil.

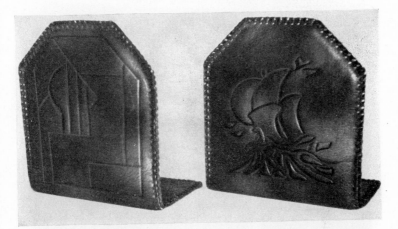

Fig. 123. Book Ends

BOOK END

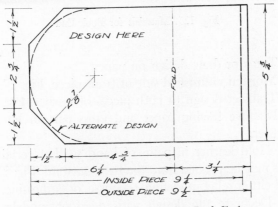

DESIGN HERE

FOLD

ALTERNATE DESIGN

Fig. 124. Working Drawing for Book End

(3) Remove patterns and cut out leather pieces on outline with sharp scissors, Fig. 25.

(4) Mark size of front piece on durable tracing paper.

(5) Select or create appropriate design. See section on Designs, at back of book.

Fig. 125. Materials for Book End

(6) Trace or draw design on paper.

(7) Moisten unfinished side of front piece, Fig. 27.

(8) Transfer design to both pieces of leather, Fig. 28.

(9) Remove tracing paper and press pattern lines firmly into leather.

(10) Hold leather in palm of hand so that certain raised portions may be pressed from the back outward, Fig. 126. This is called either relief modeling, repousse, or embossing.

(11) Decorate the design with deerfoot modeler in the usual manner, Figs. 44 and 45.

(12) Allow raised portions to dry and then apply rubber cement on the back side of the raised portions, Fig. 127.

(13) Place a small bit of cotton or kapok in the raised portion on the reverse side where it has just been cemented, Fig. 128. This helps hold the raised portion more rigid.

Fig. 126. Pressing for a Relief, Respousse,
or Embossed Design

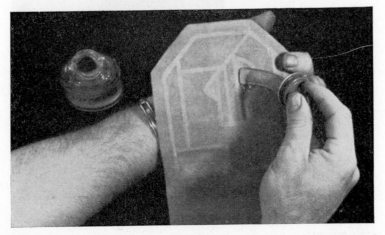

Fig. 127. Applying Rubber Cement to Back Side of the Raised Portion of
Design

(14) Apply rubber cement to the face side of the metal form, Fig. 129.

(15) Place metal form on a thin, smooth sheet of cotton and allow to dry a few minutes, Fig. 130.

Fig. 128. Placing Cotton on the Back Side of the Raised Portions

Fig. 129. Applying Cement to Metal Form for Padding

(16) Trim surplus cotton from the edges of metal form with scissors.

(17) Skive inside edges of both pieces of leather, Fig. 31.

(18) Apply rubber cement along skived edges, Fig. 32.

(19) Place metal form in proper position on the outside piece of leather, and then place inside piece in relative position, Fig. 121.

Fig. 130. Placing Cemented Form on Cotton

(20) Press cemented edges firmly together to conform with bends on form, Fig. 121.

(21) Trim irregularities of assembled piece—allow $\frac{3}{16}$ inch of leather beyond form for lacing, Fig. 122.

(22) Color edges with India ink, Fig. 35.

(23) Punch edges for lacing, Fig. 36.

(24) Lace edges with buttonhole stitch, Figs. 46–49 and 79. Start lacing at bottom for splicing.

(25) Roll laced edges, Fig. 52.

(26) Clean with saddle soap and polish, Figs. 38 and 39.

9.

Zipper Notebook Brief Case

THE ZIPPER NOTEBOOK BRIEF CASE is the most advanced and expensive of the projects; it embodies many of the essential operations and in addition entails several new ones. It is the most expensive project because of the large amount of leather required to make the cover, lining, and pockets. The long-length zipper is another item to be considered when the cost is computed. In comparison to similar commercial products, however, the craftsman will find the total expense well spent.

It is a case to be desired by any student or draftsman, especially for the person who has constant use for such an article. It will last indefinitely and wear well.

The ring plate may be procured from an old discarded notebook, and if the rivets are useless, split rivets will suffice. .

A type of wide lacing known as Venetian lacing is introduced in this project because it is especially suitable for large projects.

The effectiveness of the zipper opening may be enhanced by the addition of the thong pull to aid in opening and closing the case.

The designs may be personalized by adding a monogram.

Fig. 131. Zipper Notebook Brief Case,
Closed

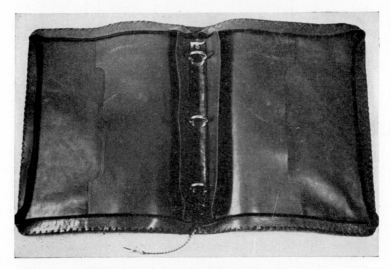

Fig. 132. Zipper Notebook Brief Case, Open

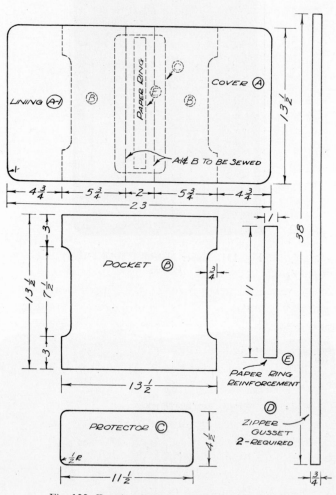

Fig. 133. Drawing for Zipper Notebook Brief Case

ZIPPER NOTEBOOK BRIEF CASE

Materials required (Fig. 134):

Quantity	Material	Size
1	Tooling calfskin, mottled steerhide, or cowhide A	13½ x 23
1	Skiving lining A–1	13½ x 23
1	Tooling calfskin or mottled steerhide B	13½ x 13½
1	Tooling calfskin or mottled steerhide C	4½ x 11½
2	Tooling calfskin or mottled steerhide D	¾ x 38
1	Cowhide E	1 x 11
1	Florentine lacing—wide	7⁄16 x 200
1	Paper ring plate	2 or 3 ring
1	Zipper	36 inch
2	Edge lace—bevel edges (contrasting colors)	3⁄32 x 12
	Necessary rivets for ring plate	
	Mercerized thread	No. 40
	India ink	
	Rubber cement	
	Saddle soap	

Essential tools (Fig. 12):

cement applier (*15*), center punch, dye brush (*18*), lacing gauge punch (*1*), mallet (*13*), paper clips, scissors (*2*), sewing machine, sheepskin polisher (*14*), sponge, stippler (*11*), square (*5*), tin snips (*3*), tracer and deerfoot modeler (*9*), and waxing cloth.

Order of procedure:

(1) Draw and cut out patterns or mark off directly on the smooth side of the leather.

(2) Cut out pieces with sharp scissors. Use tin snips for cutting cowhide strip for reinforcement.

(3) Select or create appropriate design. See section on Designs, at back of book.

(4) Moisten rough side of cover piece for tooling, Fig. 27.

(5) Transfer design to cover piece, Fig. 28.

(6) Remove paper design and press lines firmly into leather.

(7) Decorate design with deerfoot modeler, Figs. 44 and 45, and stipple if desired.

(8) Place ring plate in proper position on pieces C, B, and E, respectively. See Fig. 133 and Fig. 135.

(9) Mark and punch rivet holes with lacing gauge punch.

(10) Insert rivets through E, B, C, and metal ring plate and rivet with center punch, Fig. 135, so that rivet spreads.

(11) Locate and cement pocket B to lining A–1.

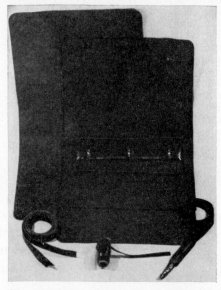

Fig. 134. Materials for Zipper Notebook
Brief Case

(12) Sew A–1 to B close on either side of paper ring plate. This serves a two-fold purpose: first, to form bottoms of pockets; and second, to form back of notebook.

(13) Apply rubber cement along the outside of the unfinished surfaces of cover and lining.

(14) Press lining firmly to cover.

(15) Apply rubber cement to zipper tape and to unfinished surfaces of zipper gussets D.

(16) Press zipper gussets firmly to zipper; allow an inch at each end of the gusset and sufficient space for the zipper to be opened and closed.

(17) Sew zipper to the gussets with sewing machine.

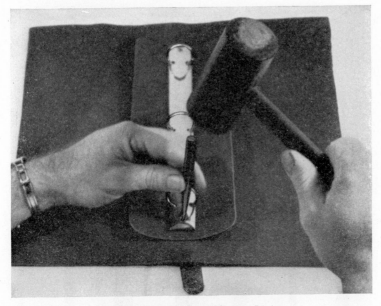

Fig. 135. Riveting Ring Plate to Lining

(18) Apply rubber cement along opposite edge of unfinished surfaces of gussets D which have not been sewed to zipper tape, and also on the glazed surface of the skived lining. This is preparation for aligning gussets to the assembled case.

(19) Press gussets firmly to the case.

(20) Trim irregularities of assembled parts.

(21) Color edges with India ink.

(22) Crease edges which will not be laced.

(23) Punch edges for lacing. These holes should be ⅜ between centers to take care of wide Venetian lacing.

(24) Lace the projects with simple Venetian edge lacing. This is similar to whip stitch.

(25) Clean and polish with saddle soap.

VENETIAN LACING

Fig. 136 Detail of Venetian Lacing

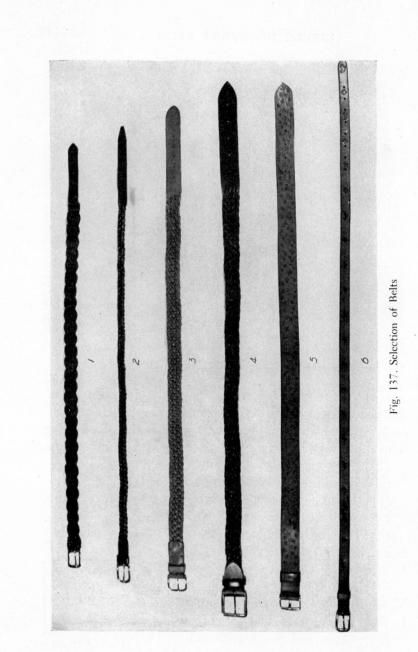

Fig. 137. Selection of Belts

144

10.

Belts

Aɴʏ ᴏꜰ ᴛʜᴇ ʙᴇʟᴛꜱ shown in Fig. 137 may be made by following the operations for the three projects taken up in this

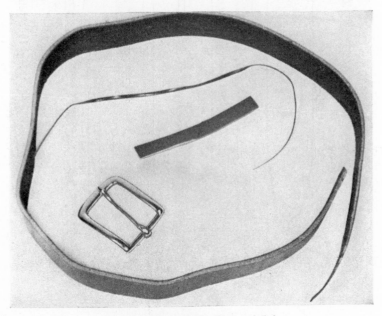

Fig. 138. Materials for Stamped Belt

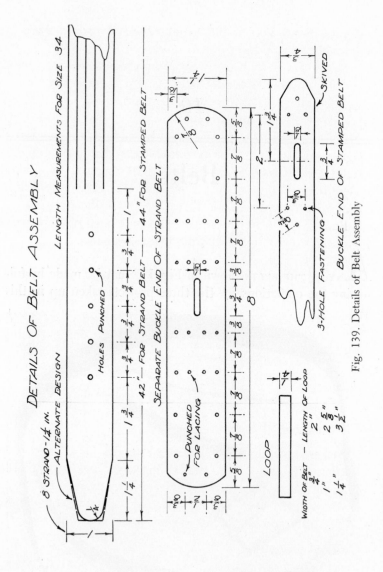

Fig. 139. Details of Belt Assembly

146

chapter. Some are suitable for boys and men, while others are desirable for girls and women.

Belt *1*, Fig. 137, is easily made by utilizing scrap materials and it can produce a novelty effect if a variety of leather, as well as colors, is used in the many links. This type of belt is popular with girls and women.

Belts 2, 3, and 4, Fig. 137, involve braiding in either five- or eight-strand design. The second project describes and illustrates extensively the various processes required for making these belts. Belt 2 will prove popular with girls if the leather is in such colors as red and blue.

Belts 5 and 6 have stamped and embossed designs, made with the stamps and embossing wheels available.

STAMPED BELT

Materials required (Fig. 138):

Quantity	Material	Size
1	Stamping cowhide	¾ x 44
1	Tooling calfskin or thin cowhide	¼ x 2
1	Edge lace—bevel edge	3/32 x 12
1	Belt buckle	¾
	Rubber cement	
	Oxalic acid—10% solution in water	
	Saddle soap	

Essential tools (Fig. 12):

background stamps (*23*), cement applier (*15*), draw gauge (*19*), edge creaser (*24*), embossing wheel and carriage (*12*), lacing gauge punch (*1*), mallet (*13*), scissors (*2*), sheepskin polisher (*14*), skiving knife (*7*), square or straightedge (*5*), stamping block, and waxing cloth.

Order of procedure:

(1) Mark for width and cut cowhide for belt strap. This procedure should start by cutting the first two or three inches with a knife and straightedge and then finishing with a draw gauge, Fig. 140.

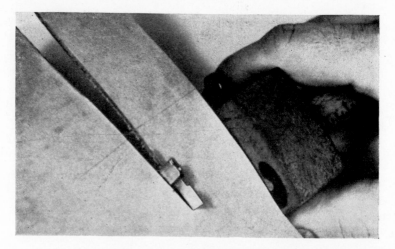

Fig. 140. Cutting Cowhide with Draw Gauge

(2) Submerge leather strip in water for an instant; then wrap in damp cloth or paper and allow to remain about one hour.

(3) Remove belt from wrapping and crease edge heavily with a belt edge creaser, Fig. 141.

(4) Emboss the edges next to the crease with embossing wheel and carriage, Fig. 142. Use straightedge for even, straight line.

(5) Select and stamp a desirable design from the available background stamps.

(6) After the belt has dried, mark and punch hole for belt buckle.

(7) Cut, crease, and skive ends of belt loop.

(8) Fasten ends of loop with eyelet. Same size and type as used for holding key plate in place is excellent.

(9) Skive back about 1½ inches on the rough surface of the buckle end of the belt.

(10) Apply rubber cement to skived portion of belt and to that portion of the belt to which it will be fastened.

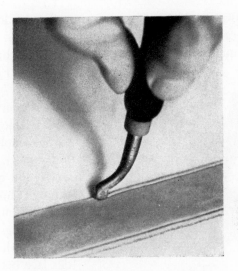

Fig. 141. Creasing the Edge of a Belt

Fig. 142. Embossing with Wheel and Carriage

(11) Insert buckle and loop. See drawing for locations.

(12) Press cemented portions firmly together.

(13) Punch holes and fasten the buckle with the three-hole

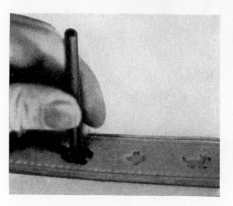

fastening, Figs. 139 and 144.

(a) Insert lace from back side of belt through holes 2 and 3, Fig. 144–A.

(b) Put end a down through hole 1, and bring it up through hole 2, Fig. 144–B.

(c) Push end b under lace between holes 1 and 3, Fig. 144–B.

Fig. 143. Stamping a Design

THREE-HOLE BELT FASTENING

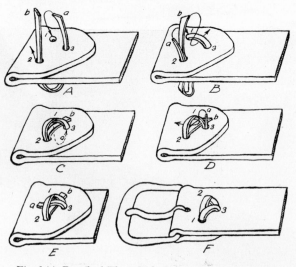

Fig. 144. Detail of Three-Hole Belt or Buckle Fastening

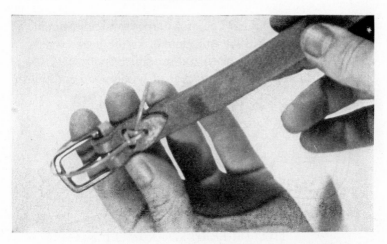

Fig. 145. Reverse Side of Three-Hole Belt Fastening

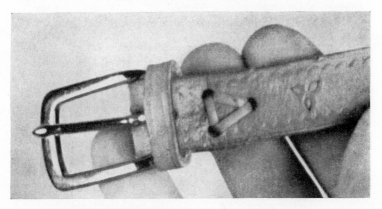

Fig. 146. Front Side of Three-Hole Belt Fastening

(d) Insert end *a* down through hole 1 again, Fig. 144–C.

(e) Bring end *a* up through hole 3, Fig. 144–D.

(f) Push end *a* underneath the lace which goes from holes 1 to 2, Fig. 144–D and 144–E. See also Fig. 145.

(g) Cut off surplus lace. Front side of fastening should look like Fig. 144–F and Fig. 146.

(14) Mark and punch holes for proper waist adjustment.

(15) Clean with 10% solution of oxalic acid crystals in water. Apply with clean cloth and rub soiled spots.

(16) When it is dry, apply coat of saddle soap and polish.

FIVE-STRAND BELT

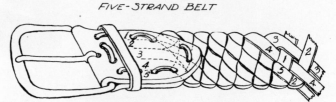

Fig. 147. Design for Five-Strand Belt

FIVE- OR EIGHT-STRAND BELT

Materials required for eight-strand belt, Size 34 (Fig. 149):

Quantity	Material	Size
1	Cowhide—shoulder piece preferred	1¼ x 42
1	Cowhide	1¼ x 8
1	Tooling calfskin or thin cowhide	¼ x 3½
1	Belt buckle	1¼
1	Edge lace—bevel edge	³⁄₃₂ x 18
	Rubber cement	
	Oxalic acid—10% solution in water	
	Saddle soap	

DESIGN OF EIGHT-STRAND BELT

Fig. 148. Design for Eight-Strand Belt

Essential tools (Fig. 12):

cement applier (15), draw gauge (19), edge creaser (24), lacing gauge punch (1), scissors (2), sheepskin polisher (14), skiving knife (7), square or straightedge (5), and waxing cloth.

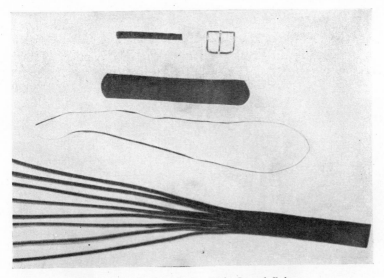

Fig. 149. Materials for Eight-Strand Belt

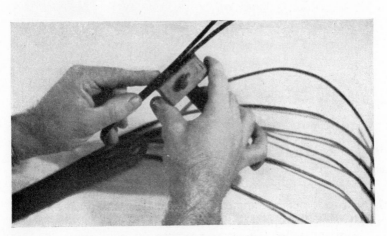

Fig. 150. Cutting Belt Strands with Draw Gauge

Order of procedure:

(1) Mark and cut cowhide for belt strap, Fig. 140.

(2) Measure and mark the strap into eight equal parts for stripping.

Fig. 151. Braiding First Strand in Belt Making

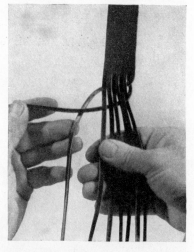

Fig. 152. Braiding Second Strand in Belt Making

(3) Strip or cut the strap into eight equal parts with the draw gauge, Fig. 150. Cut all but 7 inches which is to serve as the tongue of the belt.

(4) Nail or fasten securely the solid end or the tongue of the belt to some convenient working surface. A vertical surface permits easier handling of the strands.

(5) Braid the strands, Figs. 151–154:

(a) Number the strands from right to left.

(b) Pass strand 1 over strand 2, under 3, over 4, under 5, over 6, under 7, and over 8, Figs. 148 and 151.

(c) Pass strand 2 over 3, under 4, over 5, under 6, over 7, and under 8, Fig. 152.

Fig. 153. Braiding Third Strand in Belt Making

Fig. 154. Ends of Strands Tied

(d) Now pass strand 1 under 2 and pull it back into line parallel to strand 8, Fig. 152.

(e) Pass strand 3 over 4, under 5, over 6, under 7, over 8, and under 1, Fig. 153.

(f) Now pass strand 2 under strand 3 and pull it back into line next to strand 1, parallel with it, Fig. 153.

(g) Continue this series of operations until the belt has been completely braided, Fig. 154.

Fig. 155. Skiving Ends of Strands

Fig. 156. Cementing Strands on Buckle Strap

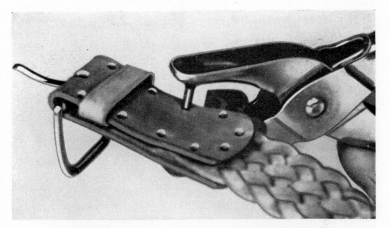

Fig. 157. Punching Holes for Strand-Buckle End Fastening

(h) Tie the ends of the strands to keep them from raveling and check for length measurement, Fig. 154.

(6) Find length of the belt by encircling the waist.

(7) Skive 1½ inches of the unfinished surfaces of the remaining strands.

(8) Cut out the remaining parts for the belt.

(9) Locate and punch slot for the buckle. See drawing.

(10) Apply rubber cement to both surfaces of all the strands and to the unfinished surfaces of the buckle end strap.

(11) Crease the edges of the belt loop.

(12) Skive the ends of the loop and fasten them together with eyelet. Size of the buckle loop is determined by pressing it around double thickness of the belt.

(13) Insert the buckle and slip the loop on the buckle end.

(14) Pull the strands closely together and press them in their proper place on the buckle strap.

(15) Press the buckle strap over the cemented ends of the braided section. Fig. 157 shows the end pressed over.

(16) Mark and punch the holes for lacing, Fig. 157. Obtain dimensions from drawing, Fig. 139.

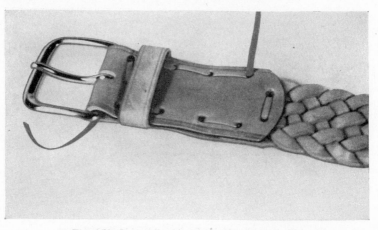

Fig. 158. Lacing Buckle End to Braided Section

(17) Lace the buckle section to the braided part, Fig. 158. The lacing procedure consists of an in-and-out stitch through the perforations, Fig. 158. The lacing is terminated by tucking the ends between the two layers of leather.

(18) Mark and punch the holes for the correct waist adjustment. The approximate measurements will be found on Fig. 139.

(19) Crease the edges of the tongue end of the belt, Fig. 141.

(20) Clean the leather with a 10% solution of oxalic acid.

(21) Apply saddle soap and polish.

LADIES' LINK BELT

Materials required for link belt, Size 30 (Fig. 160):

Quantity	Material	Size
29	Tooling calfskin or mottled steerhide (links)	1 x 2⅞
1	Tooling calfskin or mottled steerhide	¾ x 6
1	Tooling calfskin or mottled steerhide	¼ x 3
1	Belt buckle	¾
1	Snap-button assembly	⅜
	India ink	
	Rubber cement	
	Saddle soap	

Essential tools (Fig. 12):

cement applier (*15*), dye brush (*18*), edge creaser (*24*), lacing gauge punch (*1*), scissors (*2*), skiving knife (*7*), sheepskin polisher (*14*), snap-setting outfit (*22*), and waxing cloth.

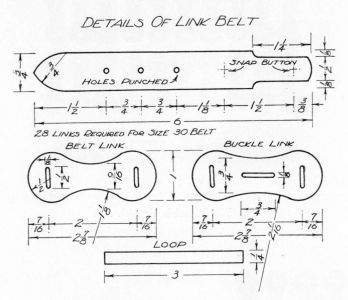

Fig. 159. Working Drawing for Link Belt

Order of procedure:

(1) Draw and cut out the patterns. See Fig. 159.

(2) Place templates on leather and mark around with a sharp pencil. Note the possible use of scrap stock, Fig. 161.

(3) Cut the leather on the marked lines, Fig. 25.

(4) Mark and punch holes to form the slots in the links, Figs. 66 and 67.

(5) Mark location for snap-button assembly on the belt tongue. Measurements will be found in drawing, Fig. 159.

(6) Punch holes and assemble snap buttons, Figs. 54–58.

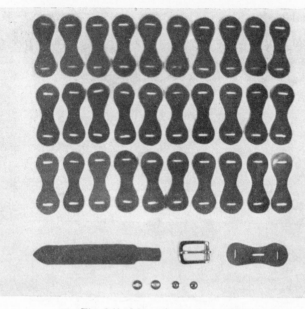

Fig. 160. Materials for Link Belt

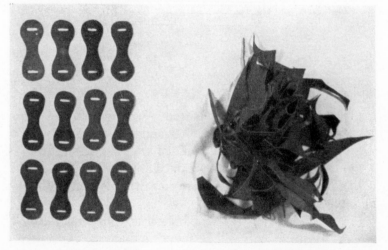

Fig. 161. Utilizing Scrap Leather for Belt Links

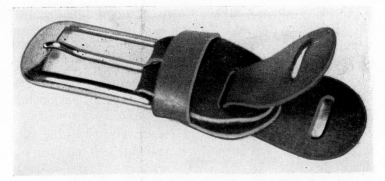

Fig. 162. Inserting Buckle into the Buckle Link

(7) Color edges with India ink, Fig. 35.

(8) Insert the buckle into the buckle link, Fig. 162.

(9) Skive the ends of the belt loop, Fig. 31.

(10) Apply rubber cement on the skived ends of loop, Fig. 32.

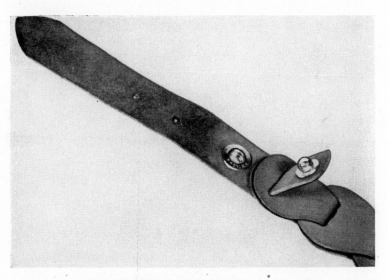

Fig. 163. Assembling the Tongue End to a Link Belt

(11) Press the cemented ends of the loop firmly together, Fig. 33. Size of the loop is determined by pressing it around a double thickness of the belt tongue.

(12) Slip the belt loop through the buckle link so that the loop is on the front side next to the buckle.

(13) Insert a belt link through the slots of the buckle link, Fig. 162.

(14) Continue the linking procedure until all of the links have been connected or until the desired length has been obtained, Fig. 162.

(15) Insert the snap-button end of the tongue through the slots of the last link and snap shut, Fig. 163.

(16) Apply saddle soap and polish, Figs. 38 and 39.

11.

Boy-Scout Accessories

$\mathbf{F}$IG. 164 ILLUSTRATES four of the more common projects thought of in connection with Boy Scouts and their activities. These are by no means the only Scout projects or problems, but they do have particular significance to the Scout.

The thong hatband is very flexible in its applications. It may be made into a hat band, belt, zipper pull, or watch fob by controlling the length of plaiting. Any problem will be all the more interesting if two contrasting colors of leather are used. When the thong is used as a belt, a sliding knot may be employed for making correct belt adjustment. This same thong, when made in shorter lengths, is ideal for Boy-Scout hatbands. This process or series of operations is also involved in making the zipper fastening. This has been referred to in the Zipper Coin-Purse Key-Case, Ladies' Zipper Handbag, and Zipper Notebook.

The neckerchief slide has an important place in Scout equipment. It is also ideal for napkin rings. The long piece of leather for making this project is cut with a draw gauge. The leather should be moistened before using; then, after it has been worked according to the procedure and has dried, it will hold its shape indefinitely.

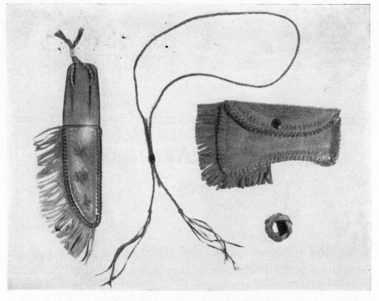

Fig. 164. Boy-Scout Accessories

The knife sheath is attractive and offers many possibilities for stamped and embossed designs. The lacing should be reinforced with copper wire to prevent the knife point and edges from cutting the lacing. This and the fringe are features not usually found on commercially manufactured sheaths. A small amount of thong work will hold the handle of the knife against the sheath when in its proper place.

The ax sheath is a companion project to the knife sheath. It, too, can be made very elaborate through the many interesting designs arising from the use of various stamping and embossing tools. The fringe of this project too is merely ornamental but enhances the general appeal of the ax sheath.

HATBAND—FOUR-PLAIT, DIAMOND-DESIGN, ROUND-THONG

Materials required:

Quantity	Material	Size
2	Tooling calfskin disks (contrasting colors)	6 inches diameter

Essential tools (Fig. 12):

compass or dividers, scissors (2), thong cutter (21), thong rolling block, and a nail.

Order of procedure:

(1) Cut two disks, 6 inches diameter, from two contrasting colors of leather, Fig. 165. (Commercial lacing may be used instead of making it by use of calfskin disks and a thong cutter.)

(2) Cut a short strip along the circumference of each disk, Fig. 165. This strip is used as a leader; it will vary according to the desired width, and ⅛ inch is suggested as satisfactory.

(3) Adjust a sharp knife or razor blade in the thong cutter for the desired width of thong, Fig. 166.

(4) Place the disk with the leader inserted under the cutting knife, Fig. 166.

(5) Pull the leader gently with one hand while holding the cutter with the other hand, Fig. 166. The leather disk revolves by itself as a continuous thong is formed.

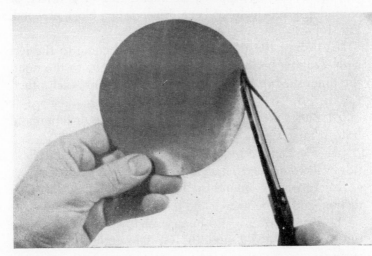

Fig. 165. Cutting Leader Strip on Disk

Fig. 166. Cutting the Thong

(6) Braid the four-plait round thong, Fig. 167.

(a) Insert two thongs *ad* and *bc*, of contrasting colors through either the zipper attachment, ring of a swivel, or around a spike which has been driven into a block of wood, Fig. 167–A.

(b) Adjust the thongs so that *ad* will come to the left with *d* falling between ends *b* and *c*. Bring *bc* to the right; the unfinished or flesh sides should fall against each other, Fig. 167–B.

(c) Pass *a* around the back in a clockwise direction and bring it up between *b* and *c*, Fig. 167–C.

(d) Place end *a* over *b* and against *d*, so that the flesh sides will come together as in Figs. 167–D and 167–E.

(e) Pass end *c* around the back in a counterclockwise direction, and up between *a* and *d*, Fig. 167–E.

(f) Bring *c* over *a* and up against *b* with the flesh sides together, Figs. 167–F and 167–G. This completes the first cycle.

(g) Pass d, which is on the far left, in a clockwise direction around the back and up between b and c, Fig. 167–G. This step begins the second cycle.

FOUR-PLAIT ROUND THONG

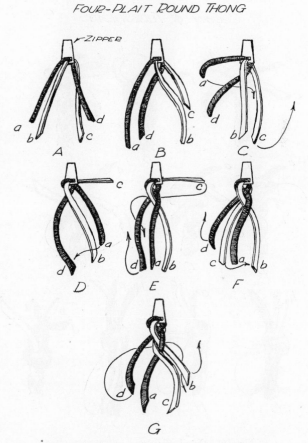

Fig. 167. Detail of Four-Plait Round Thong

(h) Bring d over c and against a with the flesh sides together.

(j) Pass b around the back in a counterclockwise direction and up between a and d.

(k) Bring *b* over *d* and against *c*, with the flesh sides together. This completes the second cycle by using all four ends for the plaiting procedure. It will be noticed that a diamond weave is being formed, and, at the completion of

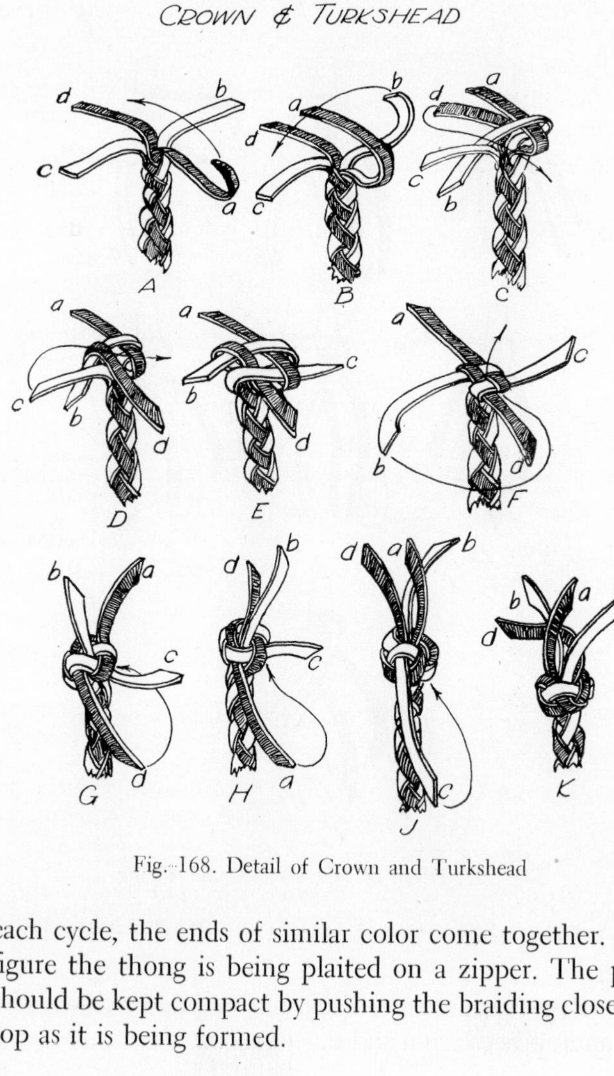

CROWN & TURKSHEAD

Fig. 168. Detail of Crown and Turkshead

each cycle, the ends of similar color come together. In this figure the thong is being plaited on a zipper. The pattern should be kept compact by pushing the braiding close to the top as it is being formed.

(1) Continue the pattern procedure until a sufficient length has been plaited to go around the waist with an ample surplus for forming the crown and turkshead and for tying.

(7) Form the crown and turkshead to terminate the plaiting, Fig. 168.

(a) Hold the plaiting with the four loose strands pointing up so that the similarly colored ends a and d fall apart opposite each other and ends b and c do likewise, Fig. 168–A. The flesh side should be up.

(b) Loop end a over next to d, Figs. 168–A and 168–B.

(c) Loop end b over a so that it falls next to c, Fig. 168–B.

(d) Loop end d over b so that it is opposite a, Figs. 168–C and 168–D.

(e) Loop end c over d and through the loop formed by a, Figs. 168–D and 168–E.

(f) Pull all four strands compactly, but not too tight, to form the crown, Figs. 168–E and 168–F.

(g) Open the crown sufficiently with a tracer modeler so that end b may be swung under d and come up through the center opening of the crown, Figs. 168–F and 168–G.

(h) Swing d under c and up through the center of the crown, Figs. 168–G and 168–H.

(j) Swing a under b and up through the center of the crown, Fig. 168–H.

(k) Swing c under a and up through the center of the crown, Fig. 168–J. This process roughly forms the turkshead, Fig. 168–K.

(l) Adjust the strands in the turkshead so that the flesh sides will be out, and pull the knot firm which has just been formed, Fig. 168–K.

(8) The opposite end of the thong belt is made into a crown and turkshead by the same procedure. Cut the strands from the

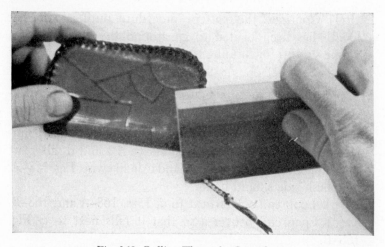

Fig. 169. Rolling Thong for Smoothness

nail or spike, ravel the end about four or five inches, and re-
peat the above series of steps.

(9) Roll the plaited strand or thong under a rolling block
or board to smooth out any unevenness and to equalize the
tension on the strands, Fig. 169.

SLIDING KNOT

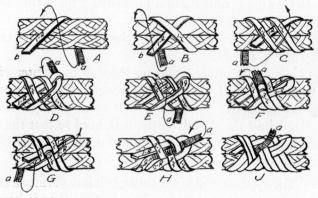

Fig. 170. Detail of Sliding Knot

(10) Form the sliding knot, Figs. 170 and 171. This is to take the place of a buckle for adjustment of length.

(a) Hold the thongs of the belt doubled, and place the lacing with the short end *b* to the left, Fig. 170–A. This is the beginning of spiral 1-right, to be called 1–R.

(b) Bring end *a* up and over *b* and around the back of the belt, Figs. 170–A and 170–B. This forms spiral 1-left, to be called 1–L.

(c) Bring *a* up and over *b* again and around the back, parallel to that done in step (b), Figs, 170–B and 170–C. This forms spiral 2–L. Sufficient space has been left between the two spirals for a third one to be done later.

(d) Bring *a* up over spirals 1–L and 2–L, and insert it under spiral 1–R, thus forming spiral 2–R, Figs 170–C and 170–D.

(e) Bring *a* around the back and up between spirals 1–L and 2–L, over spiral 2–R and under spiral 1–R, Figs. 170–D and 170–E.

Fig. 171. Making the Sliding Knot

(f) Bring a around the back to start spiral 3–R, Fig. 170–F. This completes the first cycle.

(g) This step begins the second cycle. Follow steps (a) to (f), using the identical procedure. Figs. 170–G, 170–H, and 170–J picture the start of the cycle, which parallels the first.

(h) End the sliding knot, cutting off surplus lacing.

NECKERCHIEF SLIDE

Materials required:

Quantity	Material	Size
1......	Cowhide....................................	³⁄₁₆ x 36

Essential tools (Fig. 12):

dowel, ¾ inch diameter, or broom handle, draw gauge (19), tracer modeler (8).

Fig. 172. Neckerchief Slide

Order of procedure:

(1) Mark and cut piece of cowhide with the draw gauge, Fig. 140.

(2) Submerge the leather strip in water for a few minutes; then wrap in a damp cloth and allow to remain for at least fifteen minutes.

NECKERCHIEF SLIDE

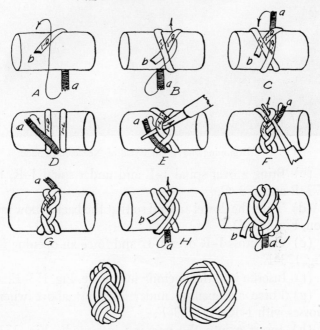

Fig. 173. Details of Neckerchief Slide

(3) Form the three-strand, five-spiral slide, Fig. 173:

(a) Place the strip of leather over the dowel forming a right spiral, 1–R, with the short end *b* on the front left, Fig. 173–A.

(b) Bring end *a* up to the left and over *b*, forming a left spiral, called 1–L, Figs. 173–A and 173–B.

Fig. 174. Beginning the Third Cycle of Neckerchief Slide

(c) Bring a over spiral 1–L and under spiral 1–R, Figs. 173–B and 173–C.

(d) Turn the dowel around so that the back is now facing you, Fig. 173–D.

(e) Crisscross 1–R over 1–L, and force an opening for a, Fig. 173–E.

(f) Insert a into the opening just made, Fig. 173–E.

(g) Force an opening under 1–L just above where it crosses with 1–R, Fig. 173–F.

(h) Insert a into the opening just made, Fig. 173–G. This completes the first cycle.

(j) Turn the dowel back again to its original position, Fig. 173–H.

(k) Start the second cycle by working parallel to 2–R as shown in Fig. 173–C. Continue with steps (c) to (h), inclusive. Fig. 174 shows the beginning of the third cycle.

(l) Start the third cycle in the same manner as explained in step (k).

(m) Cut off surplus ends of *a* and *b* when the third cycle has been completed. Tuck the ends inside the slide.

(4) Allow the slide to dry thoroughly; then remove it from the dowel. It is now ready for use.

KNIFE SHEATH

Materials required (Fig. 177):

Quantity	Material	Size
1	Stamping cowhide A	2¼ x 9½
1	Stamping cowhide B	2¼ x 6
1	Suede or calfskin C	2¼ x 6½
1	Edge lacing or cut thong	3⁄32 x 40
1	Enameled copper wire—26-gauge	18 inch
	Rubber cement	
	Saddle soap	

Fig. 175. Knife Sheath

Essential tools (Fig. 12):

background stamping tools (*23*), cement applier (*15*), edge creaser (*24*), lacing gauge punch (*1*), mallet (*13*), scissors (*2*), skiving knife (*7*), sheepskin polisher (*14*), stamping block, tin snips (*3*), and waxing cloth.

Order of procedure:

(1) Draw and cut out templates or patterns.

(2) Place templates on leather and mark around with a sharp pencil.

(3) Cut out the pieces with tin snips, Fig. 178.

(4) Submerge pieces A

and *B* in water for a minute; then wrap them in a damp cloth and allow to stand for at least one hour.

(5) Select a desirable design from the available background stamps and embossing wheels.

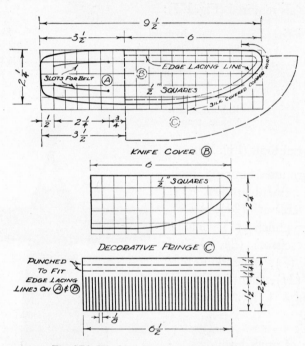

Fig. 176. Working Drawing of Knife Sheath

(6) Crease the edges which will not be laced.

(7) Stamp the desired design on pieces *A* and *B* while they are still damp.

(8) After the leather has dried, mark the location for the belt slots.

(9) Punch holes at the extremities of the marking for slots.

(10) Cut the slots with the skiving knife.

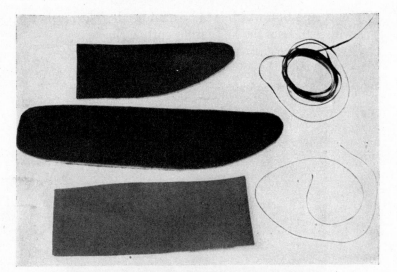

Fig. 177. Materials Required for Knife Sheath

(11) Skive the edges of the unfinished surface of B and along the finished surface of A, to which B will be laced.

(12) Mark and cut the fringe with scissors on piece C.

(13) Apply a narrow strip of cement along the skived edges of A and B and on both surfaces of the uncut portion of fringe piece C.

(14) Place C in its proper position on A, over which B is pressed firmly.

(15) Punch the edges for lacing, Fig. 36.

(16) Punch an additional line of holes on the fringe piece C just off the edge of the sheath proper. These holes should correspond to the holes on the sheath, and are for the purpose of lacing through the fringe piece.

(17) Lace the edges with the buttonhole stitch, Figs. 46–49 and 79.

(18) Roll the laced edges with a mallet.

(19) Reinforce the laced edges with copper wire, which is laced similarly to the cobbler's stitch, Fig. 71. Refer to Fig.

176 for the portion which is to be reinforced. The purpose of this wire is to keep the knife from cutting the lacing.

(20) Apply coat of saddle soap and polish.

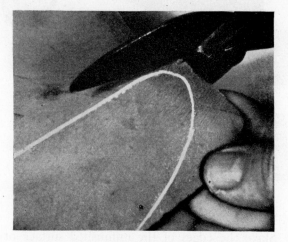

Fig. 178. Cutting Leather with Tin Snips

AX SHEATH

Materials required (Fig. 181):

Quantity	Material	Size
1	Stamping cowhide A	6½ x 8
1	Stamping cowhide B	4 x 8
1	Suede or calfskin C	4½ x 5½
1	Edge lace or cut thong	³⁄₃₂ x 140
1	Snap-button assembly	½
	Rubber cement	
	Saddle soap	

Essential tools (Fig. 12):

background stamping tools (23), cement applier (15), edge creaser (24), lacing gauge punch (1), mallet (13), scissors (2), sheepskin polisher (14), snap-setting outfit (22), stamping block, tin snips (3), and waxing cloth.

Fig. 179. Ax Sheath

Order of procedure:

(1) Draw and cut out patterns.

(2) Place templates on leather and mark around them with a sharp pencil.

(3) Cut out the pieces.

(4) Submerge pieces A and B in water for a few minutes; then wrap them in a damp cloth and allow to stand for at least one hour.

(5) Select a desirable design from the available background stamps and embossing wheels.

(6) Crease the edges, which will not be laced.

(7) Stamp the desired design on pieces A and B while they are still damp.

(8) After the leather has dried, mark the location for the belt slots.

(9) Punch holes at the extremities of the marking for slots.

(10) Cut the slots with the skiving knife.

(11) Mark and cut the fringe with scissors on piece C.

(12) Apply a narrow strip of rubber cement along the inner edges of the unfinished surfaces of A and B and on both sur-

BOY SCOUT AX SHEATH

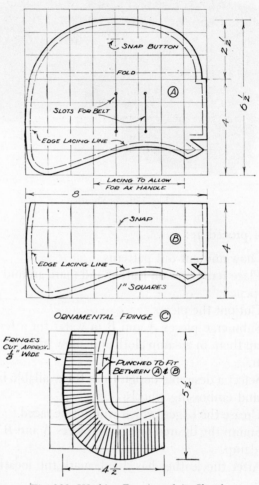

Fig. 180. Working Drawing of Ax Sheath

faces of the uncut portion of fringe C. The cement is to be applied only to those edges which are to be laced.

(13) Place C in its proper position on A over which B is pressed firmly.

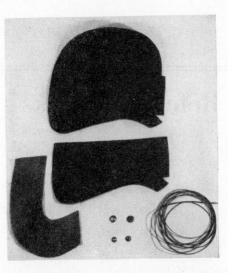

Fig. 181. Materials Required for Ax Sheath

(14) Punch the edges for lacing, Fig. 36.

(15) Punch an additional line of holes on the fringe piece C just off the edge of the main sheath proper. These holes should correspond to the holes on the sheath and are for the purpose of lacing through the fringe piece.

(16) Lace the edges with the buttonhole stitch. An opening should be allowed in the bottom of the sheath for the ax handle.

(17) Roll the laced edges with a mallet.

(18) Mark location, punch holes, and assemble snap button.

(19) Apply saddle soap and polish.

Reference Books

Cherry, Raymond, *General Leathercraft*. McKnight and McKnight, Bloomington, Illinois, 1940

Cramlet, R. C., *Fundamentals of Leathercraft*. Bruce Publishing Company, Milwaukee, Wisconsin, 1939

Decker, M. H., *Practical Home Tanning and Fur Dressing*. Webb Book Publishing Company, St. Paul, Minnesota, 1935

Decker, M. H., *Working with Leather*. Webb Book Publishing Company, St. Paul, Minnesota, 1937

Edwards, I. M., *Practical Glove Making*. Pittman Publ. Corp., New York, 1929

Griswold, Lester, *Handicraft Simplified Procedure*. Griswold Craft School, Colorado Springs, Colorado, 1939

Hoefer, Louise C., *Design Books No. 1 and 2 for Leather*. Louise C. Hoefer, Glendale, California, 1939

Hoefer, Louise C., *Leathercraft Instructions*. Louise C. Hoefer, Glendale, California, 1939

Lemos, P. J., *Leathercraft*. School Arts Magazine Press, Worcester, Massachusetts, 1934

Mickel, Adelaide, *Leatherwork*. The Manual Arts Press, Peoria, Illinois, 1927

Roseaman, I. P., *Leather Work*. The Manual Arts Press, Peoria, Illinois, 1940

Country Hides and Skins, Bulletin No. 1055. U. S. Department of Agriculture, Bureau of Publications, Washington, D. C., 1926

Leathercraft, Merit Badge Series. Boy Scouts of America Service Library, New York, 1933

Make it of Leather. U. S. Department of Commerce, Bureau of Publications, Washington, D. C., 1933

Orange Book, The. Fellowcrafters, Boston, Massachusetts

Project in Leather. Boy Scouts of America Service Library, New York, 1933

Romance of Leather. Tanners' Council of America, New York, 1937

Story of Leather, The. The Ohio Leather Company, Girard, Ohio, 1935

Designs

Reproduced Approximately ½ Size

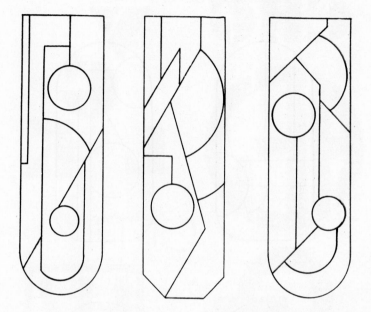

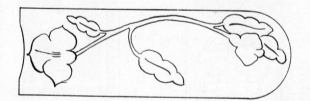

DESIGNS FOR KEY CASE

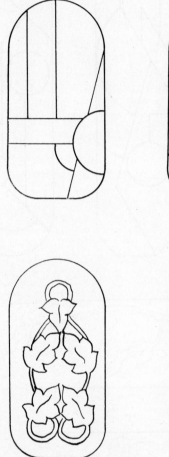

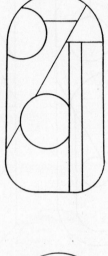

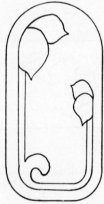

DESIGNS FOR KEY HOLDER

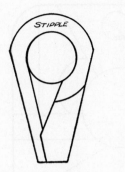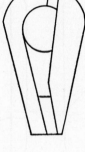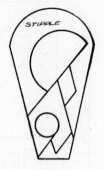

189

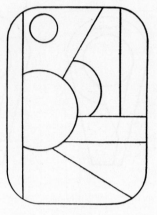

191

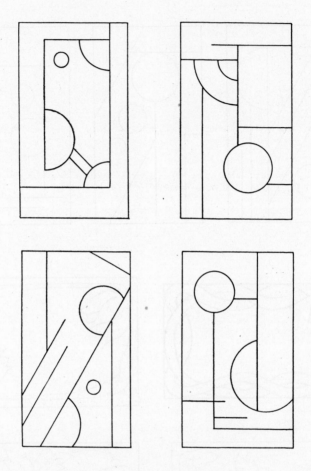

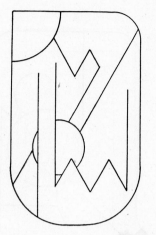

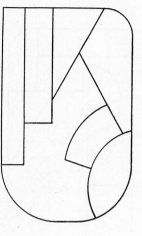

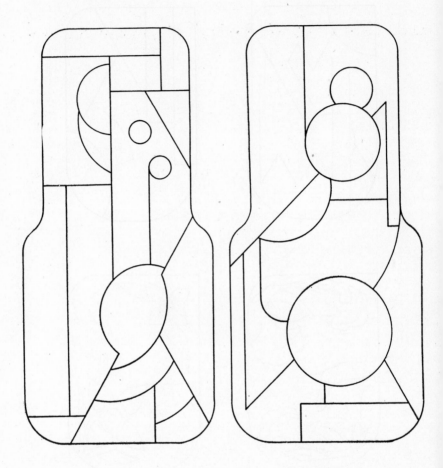

194

DESIGNS FOR LADIES' HAND BAG

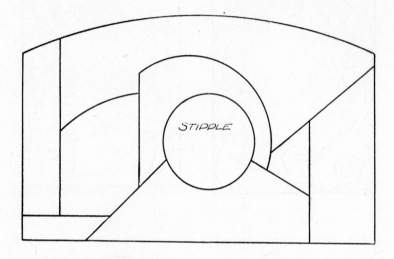

STIPPLE

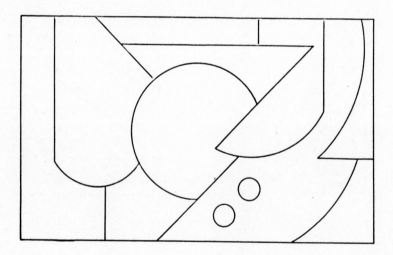

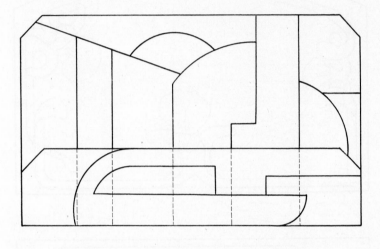

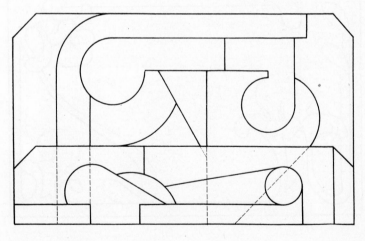

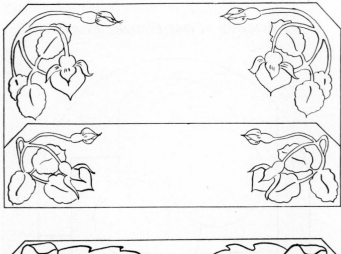

201

DESIGNS FOR BOOK ENDS

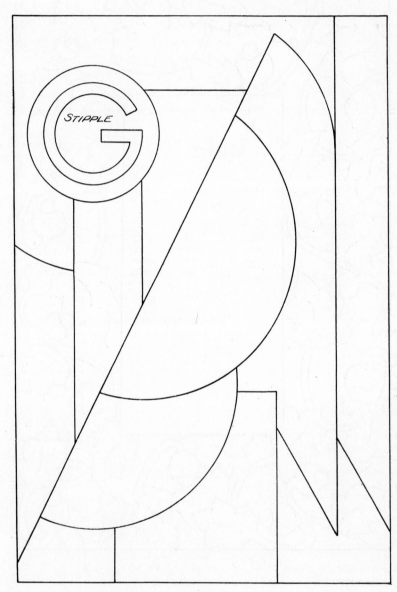

STIPPLE

Index